Call to Conscience

Call to Conscience

Jews, Judaism, and Conscientious Objection

by ALBERT S. AXELRAD

KTAV PUBLISHING HOUSE, INC.
HOBOKEN, N.J.

JEWISH PEACE FELLOWSHIP
NYACK, N.Y.

1986

Library of Congress Cataloging-in-Publication Data

Alexrad, Albert S., 1938-
  Call to conscience.

  Bibliography: p.
  1. Conscientious objectors—United States—Handbooks,
manuals, etc. 2. Conscientious objectors—Law and
legislation—United States—Handbooks, manuals, etc.
3. Peace—Religious aspects—Judaism—Handbooks, manuals,
etc. 4. Judaism—Doctrines—Handbooks, manuals, etc.
I. Title.
UB342.U5A93 1985   172'.42   85-24010
ISBN 0-88125-092-9
ISBN 0-88125-081-3 (pbk.)

MANUFACTURED IN THE UNITED STATES OF AMERICA

Dedication

To my family, which tolerated my absence and vacant-mindedness during the many months I spent on this book.

To my father, Max Axelrad, of blessed memory, an activist who struggled for a world at peace.

To my counselees—past and present—from the Brandeis University community and elsewhere, who sought my guidance on the subject of Conscientious Objection. The C.O.s I taught and advised during my rabbinic career have left me a gift in the form of the divine imperative from the Decalogue, whose words are on a poster hanging in my study:

Thou Shalt Not Kill

God

I hope I have helped them as much as I have learned from them.

To the C.O.s of all times, all nations and all wars. Their nonviolent, moral scruples show the path to peace, as reflected in the contemporary proverb:

"What if they gave a war and no one came?"

May the ranks of C.O.s expand and multiply until that evil called war is no longer a reality.

Table of Contents

Preface

My father was Max Axelrad, of blessed memory. Until his dying day in September 1960, he was a progressive activist who dreamed the dream of the biblical prophets. He dreamed of a just social order, of resources shared equitably, and above all, of a world at peace. At an early age, I too partook of his sacred visions, and it is to him and his memory that I dedicate this book. Thanks to him and the superb Jewish education that I was afforded (through the Yeshiva of Flatbush, Camp Ramah, Columbia College, the Jewish Theological Seminary of America, Hebrew Union College–Jewish Institute of America, and, most recently, Brandeis University), toiling with others in the struggle for a just world without war became a prime goal early in my life.

World War II and the Korean War punctuate my memory as a young American boy and adolescent. And with the understanding that comes with adulthood, the first war I opposed actively was the Vietnam War. While still a seminarian in 1964, I raised my voice in opposition to the war and involved myself in the peace movement.

From 1965 to 1972, as B'nai B'rith Hillel Director and Chaplain at Brandeis University, I did a great deal of draft counseling, assisting large numbers of students in their efforts to achieve conscientious objector status. This book is a direct outgrowth of that same commitment—to struggle for a just world at peace, to banish the sword from the land. The urgency of the situation on this imperiled planet of ours has only served to deepen this commitment.

My life's work is with Jews at Brandeis University. I am

writing this book to comfort and aid them and young Jews everywhere. In particular, my aim is to provide constructive counsel to those who are confronted with draft registration and do not feel they can serve in the armed forces because of their religious and moral abhorrence of violence and war. As I read the ominous world situation and the military inclinations of the current American government, I believe the reestablishment of conscription is but a step away. In the face of such an eventuality, young Americans will want and need the kind of guidance and help that this book seeks to supply.

It should be noted that this book is intended principally for the Jew. It may also, however, be of more than passing interest to adherents of other traditions for comparative purposes, for Judaism's influence on the peace aspects of other religions, and especially for the practical pointers pervading its pages.

Finally, several words of thanks are in order, and it is my pleasure to register them from the heart. First and foremost, I thank my immediate family, my wife Berta and my children, Marcy, Robin, David, and Tamar, for their understanding, good humor, and forbearance during the many hours I devoted to this work. Secondly, I wish to thank a dear friend and former student of mine, Rosalie Ripaldi Shane, who believed in me and especially in this work, giving of herself tirelessly and as a labor of love in editing this manuscript and preparing it for publication. Two other precious friends to whom I am exceedingly grateful are Judy Kaplan and Marilyn Felt, who exercised a deft hand in the earlier editing and preparation of the manuscript. My heartfelt appreciation also goes out to three colleagues, veteran draft and CO counselors whose work has received national notice. They are Robert A. Seeley of the Central Committee for Conscientious Objectors, author of the *Handbook for Conscientious Objectors*, for which this book is offered as a companion volume; Warren W. Hoover of the National Interreligious Service Board for Conscientious Objectors; and Janet Cronbach of A Separate Peace. All of these read the manuscript carefully, corroborated its technical accuracy, and suggested copious improvements. My sincere thanks also go to my Hillel colleagues, Rabbis Richard Israel, Daniel Leifer, and Laura Geller for their helpful recommendations, and especially to Reverend L. William Yolton, of the National Interreligious Service Board for Conscientious Objectors. (I credit all these for their improvements of my manuscript and take full responsibility for all its shortcomings.) I am profoundly grateful to my comrades on the national executive committee of the Jewish Peace Fellowship, especially President Naomi Goodman, Vice President Murray Polner, and Carolyn Toll for their constant encouragement and support. Lastly, my sincere and humble thanks go to my students, past and present, who have challenged me through the years and contributed to my development as a counselor to conscientious objectors.

Introduction

When a young man turns eighteen, he is required by law to register with the Selective Service. At this time there is no draft, but in a national emergency or in a state of declared or undeclared war, it could be reinstated very quickly. And the world situation being what it is, a war involving our country could erupt quite suddenly in any number of places throughout the globe. People committed to pursuing peace find it a very difficult time. Young men of registration age wonder whether to register, as the law requires, or to refuse and violate the law. It is a difficult choice. Some choose registration even though it is likely to be their first step toward entering military life. If there is another draft, every registered young man will be eligible for induction into the armed services. Others consider registration morally wrong. They believe this process is part of an escalated war consciousness that could result in armed conflict. Should a young man register or refuse? What to do?

Men who refuse to register because it goes against their moral principles have my utmost respect. Not many people are capable of civil disobedience. If this sort of noncooperation is part of a principled, ideological position, and not just a matter of self-interested draft evasion, then it has merit. When asked to offer my own advice, however, I counsel men to register. I see no efficacy in defying the law on this issue and would urge my own son to register.

If a young man is considering refusing to register for the draft, I would counsel him to get the advice of a good draft counselor, an attorney, or both. He should be well informed of

the implications and penalties involved and should not proceed mindlessly on such a course of action. Federal prosecution
of noncooperators may not happen, but if it does occur, and if
convictions are obtained, the violators may have to serve
prison terms and pay substantial fines. There is an alternative,
however, for the nonviolent, peace-pursuing person: Register
for the draft and apply for a legal exemption as a conscientious
objector.

> The draft law exempts from military service all those whose
> consciences, spurred by deeply held moral, ethical, or religious
> beliefs, would give them no rest or peace if they allowed them-
> selves to become part of an instrument of war.
> —*Welsh* v. *United States*, 398 U.S. 333 (1970)

It is for such persons, their families, and their counselors that
this book is intended.

CO Sympathizers

Conscientious objector status is an historical and legal part of
the Selective Service System. Far from being a source of embarrassment or shame, being a CO is something in which to take
pride. Many great minds, loyal citizens, and outstanding people of our nation have either been conscientious objectors or
have been sympathetic to their beliefs. Albert Einstein, a
supporter of conscientious objection, inspired the founding of
the Jewish Peace Fellowship, which promotes the cause of
nonviolence and aids conscientious objectors. Speaking of war
resisters, Einstein said (in 1953), "The existence of such a moral
elite is indispensable for the preparation of a fundamental
change in public opinion, a change that, under present day
circumstances, is absolutely necessary if humanity is to survive." The late Martin Luther King, Jr., whose birthday America now proudly celebrates, was a distinguished champion of
nonviolence. Roger Baldwin, a conscientious objector, was the
founder of the American Civil Liberties Union. Bayard Rustin,
another conscientious objector, is one of the civil rights movement's greatest leaders. A. J. Muste, famous for his book *Of*

Holy Disobedience, was a Unitarian minister prominent in the American peace movement. Much earlier, Henry David Thoreau raised an inspiring voice for nonviolence, opting for imprisonment rather than pay his taxes for the Mexican War.

President John Fitzgerald Kennedy, of blessed memory, wrote the following beautiful perspective to an old wartime friend in 1945, "War will exist until that distant day when the conscientious objector enjoys the same reputation and prestige that the warrior does today" (from Arthur Schlesinger's book, *A Thousand Days*). And in the early 19th century Daniel Webster wrote, "Where is it written in the Constitution, in what article or section is it contained, that you may take children from their parents, and parents from their children, and compel them to fight the battles of any war in which the folly or wickedness of Government may engage it?"

CO Eligibility and Status

In no way does a person's belief in nonviolence reflect cowardice, disloyalty, or evasion of responsibility to country or humankind. On the contrary, conscientious objection shows a love and compassion for one's fellow citizens and for the human family. And the law prohibits retribution or discrimination against a conscientious objector.

It used to be that membership in a traditional pacifist religious group like the Society of Friends (Quakers) was necessary to qualify one as a conscientious objector. This is no longer true. The Selective Service now acknowledges that no group has the exclusive right to have a moral opposition to war. In fact, while your claim must be religious or moral in order to be accepted, it need not be based on the moral or ethical beliefs of any specific organized religion. The term *religious* is written with a small *r* and is defined very broadly. Even if you do not belong to any organized faith, as long as you have a deep commitment to moral and ethical beliefs that guide your life as the convictions of a traditionally religious person would, you may be said to be "religious." It is important to emphasize, however, that your beliefs and values should occupy a central position in your life, mandating your behavior and actions. And if these beliefs do not allow you to participate in war, then you may be eligible for CO status.

In the past, it was necessary to affirm faith in a Supreme Being as part of a claim for becoming a conscientious objector. This is no longer true. Your claim may be based on a belief in a humanistic rather than a theistic faith. Many organized religions have humanistic or naturalistic dimensions, for that matter. Unitarianism and Ethical Culture are perfect examples of such faiths. And within the framework of Judaism, Jewish Reconstructionism is another. This school of thought was founded by the late Rabbi Mordecai M. Kaplan in the 1930s and is now a full-fledged movement along with Orthodoxy, Reform, and Conservative Judaism. Reconstructionism rejects the notion of a personal, supernatural, transcendent God. It emphasizes, instead, the concept of God as a Process, Force, or Power within the natural order of things, making for good, for morality, for love, and for fulfillment. It cannot be emphasized enough, however, that whether you are religious in a traditional sense and believe in a Supreme Being or have a more personal code of moral values, it is the sincerity, depth, strength, and pervasiveness of your beliefs that count.

Finally, since this is mainly a volume to advise Jewish COs, I must point out that in my experience Jewish applicants who base their claims on traditional religious values are more easily acceptable as conscientious objectors to the Selective Service than those whose claims are based on personal beliefs alone. Traditional Jewish values and beliefs are completely consistent with the spirit of conscientious objection and are acceptable to the Selective Service as a basis for CO status. Many outstanding rabbis and Jewish communal leaders have supported or claimed conscientious objection. Judah Magnes, the great American rabbi who went on to become the founding president of Hebrew University, heads such a list. The great German Jewish thinker, Rabbi Leo Baeck, was one whose teachings and behavior, as the famed "Rabbi of Theresienstadt," inspired the founding of the Jewish Peace Fellowship. The late Rabbi Abraham Joshua Heschel, the preeminent Jewish theologian and Jewish Theological Seminary professor, was a leading peace activist. So was the prominent Reform Rabbi Stephen S. Wise, in whose memory many synagogues have been named. Two other important Jewish voices for nonviolence, both within the framework of Orthodoxy, have been Hasidic Rabbi Joel Teitelbaum and Rabbi Aaron Soloveitchik. Others would include Rabbis Abraham Cronbach, Maurice Eisendrath, Arthur Gilbert, and Isador B. Hoffman, all of blessed memory, as well as Rabbis Immanuel Jakobovits (now chief rabbi of Great Britain), Stanley Brav, Arthur Hertzberg, Arthur Lelyveld, Roland Gittelsohn, Arnold Jacob Wolf, Balfour Brickner, David Shapiro, Jack Reimer, Henry Siegman, Robert Goldburg, Everett Gendler, Max Ticktin, Walter Wurzburger, David Wolf Silverman, Hershel Matt, Bernard Mehlman, Laura Geller, Herman Blumberg, Richard Levy, Larry Kushner, David Saperstein, Gerald Serotta, Michael Robinson, Ruth Sohn, Patricia Karlin, and Saul Berman, to name but a few. Many nonrabbinic leaders of the Jewish community have also come to be known for their peace commitments. Heading such a list are Albert Vorspan, Jane Evans, Samuel Grand, and Ira Silverman, along with many noted American Jewish personalities, including Naomi Goodman, Murray Polner, Howard Fast, Leo Pfeffer, Arthur Waskow, Carolyn Toll, and a host of others. Leading citizens of Israel, too, have also raised their voices in the cause of peace. Among the outstanding peace activists in Israel are Knesset members, other political dignitaries, former military heroes, journalists, authors, and academicians. The impressive list includes Abba Eban (M.K.), Yossi Sarid (M.K.), Shulamit Aloni (M.K.), former M.K.'s Arie (Lova) Eliav, Uri Avnery, Col. Meir Pail, and Gen. (Res.) Matti Peled, authors Natan Chofshi, Amos Oz, Avraham Ben Yehoshua, and Matti Megged, academicians Yehoshua Arielli, Shlomo Avineri, and Shimon Shamir, journalists Simha Flapan, Amos Kenan, and Avraham Burg.

Many young Jews combine the beliefs they derive directly from Judaism with their own more personal or eclectic moral beliefs in preparing their claims. Such combinations are very effective and have helped many sincere Jews achieve conscientious objector status.

Call to Conscience

The Procedure for Obtaining a Conscientious Objector Classification*

Becoming a legally recognized conscientious objector is not so difficult that any qualified young person could not follow through successfully. The whole process of getting the Selective Service System to classify you as a conscientious objector will go on for several years as each step proceeds, from before the time one registers for the draft, through preparing a claim and documenting it, receiving an induction order, and then seeking reclassification as a CO. After being classified as a CO you will be ordered to noncombatant service in the Army (1-A-O) or to alternative service (1-O), which is "civilian work in the national health, safety or interest."

Under the regulations in effect as of June 1985, you could have as little as ten days to assert your right to be classified as a CO, so getting ready to file your claim, while you have plenty of time, is very important. It would be possible for you to make a valid claim even if you have realized at the last minute your

I am deeply indebted to my comrade and colleague, Reverend L. William Yolton, executive director of the National Interreligious Service Board for Conscientious Objectors (NISBCO) in Washington, D.C., for contributing the following updated chapter. It cannot be emphasized enough that the reader is advised to consult a well-informed draft counselor or lawyer and to maintain ongoing contact with NISBCO and CCCO, so as to remain current with regard to ever changing draft and CO regulations. A.S.A.

1

convictions about being a conscientious objector to participation in war, though such a late claim may be more difficult to
prove and be accepted.

During the period of time between registration and alternative service as a CO there are many informal steps you would
want to take. You should talk over your decision with people
you trust, your family, your Hillel and/or congregational rabbi,
and a skilled draft counselor (if you can locate one). You would
want to read background material about being a CO, such as
this book and the others from the recommended bibliography
(see pp. 85-91). You might want to put on record with your
rabbi, the Jewish Peace Fellowship, and one of the national
draft-counseling organizations a record of your decision to be a
CO. You will certainly want to express your convictions
through word and deed.

Keeping a record of your activity on behalf of peace and
justice will be important for authenticating your case when
your claim is reviewed. You will want to solicit persons who
would write letters of reference on your behalf, persons who
will serve as witnesses, and even someone who could be an
adviser when you at last have your personal appearance with
the Selective Service System local claims board.

For all these records you will need to keep a file. For some of
the most important documents you collect you may even want
to maintain a duplicate file so that in an emergency someone
you trust can have access to those copies.

Here is a brief outline of the procedure: (Mandatory steps in
the Selective Service System requirements are in **bold face**.)

- Begin to think out your convictions about participation in
  war and the related issues of registration and the draft.
- Decide whether or not to register for the draft. If you do,
  then:
- **Register for the draft at a post office during the sixty days
  beginning thirty days before the eighteenth anniversary
  of your birth.**

- Document your intention to be classified as a CO from at least the time of registration, and begin a rough draft of your statement of belief, together with keeping records of your activities consistent with those beliefs.
- Check out your thinking and your understanding of the process with those you love, a religious counselor (your rabbi probably), and a draft counselor or a national counseling agency.
- **The Draft returns,** following a congressional amendment to the Military Selective Service Act which would give the president the power to resume inductions.
- **You will receive a lottery number (a "Random Sequence Number") from Selective Service,** determining the order in which you will be called when your priority group is reached in the operation of the draft.
- Make plans for finding work as a conscientious objector (alternative service) if you are opposed to noncombatant service in the Army.
- **You will receive an induction notice and classification as 1-A.**
- **Appeal the classification by requesting reclassification as a CO (1-O or 1-A-O).** Form 9 to make this request will be available at local post offices.
- **Selective Service will send you Form 22, the Claim Documentation Form—Conscientious Objector, and a notice of when you are scheduled for a personal appearance before your local claims board.**
- **Submit Form 22, together with additional documentation.** *Include (above all) a full statement of your claim to be a conscientious objector.*
- **Appear at the required personal appearance.** You may bring up to three witnesses and an adviser.
- **Selective Service will send you notice of your classification as a CO.** (You can appeal if your claim is rejected. Form 142 will specify the reasons for rejection.)
- **1-Os meet with the alternative service officer at the area**

office to negotiate an alternative service assignment. Or, 1-A-Os receive an order to induction for service as noncombatants in the Army.

- **Selective Service will send you an order to alternative service,** and comply (or appeal if the job assigned is unacceptable to your conscience).
- Service in either the Army or in alternative service will be for two years.

What to do at the Time of Registration

The special minority of COs who will not register:

For some conscientious objectors the very act of complying with the legal duty to register with the Selective Service System is a problem for their consciences. There is not an opportunity to declare your conscientious objection at the time of registration (as there once was). Some decide to register, but others find they cannot.

The relatively small number of conscientious nonregistrants, also known as "noncooperators" or "resisters," is still a significant group. Seventeen were indicted in the first four years of registration, some reached pretrial agreements with the Justice Department, others were convicted and have served brief prison sentences or longer "community service" sentences, some have had their cases dismissed, and still others have been in the courts for several years awaiting decisions on appeals. Their personal reasons of conscience have all been of the sort that probably would qualify them as conscientious objectors were they to apply at the proper time. They have strong convictions about the wrongness of the draft and the purposes it serves, which they made known to others and to the government, bringing about their indictment.

One sort of argument that the conscientious objector to the draft and registration itself would use goes like this: My conscientious beliefs do not allow me to participate in war or in preparations for war. President Carter introduced draft registration (against the advice of the Director of Selective Service) in order to send a (hostile) message to the Russians, part of the resumption of the Cold War (State of the Union address to Congress in 1980). The Director of Selective Service, General Thomas K. Turnage, has likened registration to "a powerful weapon . . . a defense weapon . . . that has a rightful place in America's arsenal alongside bombers and missiles" (Sept. 27, 1983). These officials have confirmed the situation of conscience of those who cannot thus be part of these hostilities by even so much as registering for the draft.

The Supreme Court (in *Welsh*, 1970) defined the feeling of conscientious objectors within the draft system as persons whose consciences "will give them no rest or peace if they allowed themselves to become any part of an instrument of war." Many of those who object to the draft and registration see it as an "instrument of war." Therefore, they believe they ought not to register if they are "opposed to participation in war in any form," which is the statutory definition of a conscientious objector's belief. Unfortunately, though lower-court judges have said there ought to be legal provision for those who cannot register, there is no legal way to be a conscientious objector to the draft.

The choice to be a conscientious objector to the draft itself as one of the instrumentalities of war has not only the risk of imprisonment for five years and a fine of up to $10,000, but it regularly punishes even those who have not been tried by denying them access to loans and grants for higher education. The decision to stand by one's conscience at this point can thus deny one his liberty and his education. The Solomon Amendments (after Representative Solomon of New York) requires that one be registered for the draft to be eligible for federal loans and grants for higher education. Some states and many colleges have enacted similar requirements.

Those who have taken the risk to speak out against war and the draft have been prosecuted as a consequence of the government's policy of passive prosecution. (Over four years from the initiation of registration in 1980 it finally began to go after

nonregistrants who had not identified themselves voluntarily
to the government and to others, in a policy of active prosecution.)

One of the last in this group "selectively prosecuted" by the
government is Andy Mager, who at his trial made his Jewish
religion a significant factor in his defense to the charge of
nonregistration. Andy's reasons included recognition that the
draft itself is part of the preparation to go to war, and that the
preparations for war in Central America and for nuclear war
are unjust on moral and religious grounds. He also made the
connection between the indifference of those in Nazi Germany
who knew the trains were carrying people to their deaths and
our complicity in preparations for our own holocaust. He
argued that our treaty obligations are in conflict with our
practice, and his choice was not just between a higher moral
law based on religion and positive law, but he was attempting
to follow those laws which are constitutionally binding on all
Americans. The judge said that higher laws are not relevant to
the jury's deliberation and Andy could not choose which laws
to obey. Andy was sentenced to three years in prison, but two
and a half years were suspended. (See Andy's statement in the
appendix of this book.)

The government's policy as described to the Supreme Court
is to make every effort to get the nonregistrant to register, and
the indictment will not be made if at the last moment one is
persuaded to register. Even after indictment opportunity has
been given at the pretrial stage to divert to nonpunitive process
if the person will register. Of course, these policies are subject
to change and one should not rely upon them for a last-minute
reprieve.

**The decision that most conscientious objectors make is to
register for the draft and plan to seek classification and service
as a legally recognized conscientious objector.**

The majority of conscientious objectors seem to be willing to
register for the draft, and to accept this degree of compromise
as necessary. These COs will nevertheless have to be sure that
their claims are followed up carefully, for if they are rejected at

the last stages, they too may find they must stand trial if the sincerity of their consciences is to be upheld.

If your convictions are such that you can comply with the requirement to register, the Presidential Proclamation orders you to present yourself at a post office, during the sixty days beginning thirty days before the eighteenth anniversary of your birth. There the registration cards are available on the counter or a clerk will provide you with one. Fill out the card. Though there is no section on the card to indicate at the time of registration that you intend to claim classification as a conscientious objector, you may write on the card, "I am a conscientious objector" or some similar statement. (CO counseling agencies and civil liberties advocates continue to urge provisions for COs to make official their opposition to war and to the draft at the time of registration.)

You will want to make a record of your registration, for the Selective Service has not made a place on its computer program for recording your intention to claim CO status. (It will microfilm the registration card, however.) You can make a photocopy of the form before it is submitted to the clerk, who will send it along with others collected that week for entering in the SSS computer. You can establish the date of your copy by folding it over, sealing it, and sending it to yourself; the postmark will verify the time you registered.

Selective Service will send you a form verifying your registration, and a form is included for you to correct any errors or make changes. You are to notify Selective Service of changes in address within ten days; forms for this purpose are available at local post offices.

Another way to verify your intention to claim conscientious objector status is to write Selective Service, telling them so. You may wish to state in your own words briefly your belief that you are "opposed to participation in war in any form." The law also requires you to have these beliefs based on religious training and belief, which has been broadly interpreted to include all beliefs held with the strength of conventional religious beliefs, and thus includes beliefs that some would say are "moral or ethical" in character rather than primarily "religious." You may wish to mention how your beliefs are thus founded in religious/moral/ethical training and belief. Finally, you could include a statement that you are willing to serve your country in some civilian work in the national health, safety, or interest, or in noncombatant service in the army (which are the options that the law specifies).

The support this letter to Selective Service would give your claim when you make it could be strengthened by having it notarized and by sending it "Certified Mail, Return Receipt Requested." That will tend to establish that it was really you who wrote it and sent it, and together with the receipt from the post office show when it was received by Selective Service. Selective Service will sometimes write back to say that they are not classifying COs and return your letter. That letter from SSS will also add to the records in your file attesting to your intent.

(Through all of this preliminary process you are not actually applying for the CO classification. That comes later. You will want to follow careful record keeping through all your dealings with the Selective Service System. Date all the materials you submit and file. When you speak to SSS personnel in person or by telephone, get their names and make a record summarizing what was said, and add it to your file.)

When Would the CO Claim Be Made?

CO claims cannot be made officially until draftees are actually called up for duty. (According to the regulations for inductions, this may occur only in a declared war or national emergency.) In the meantime, from before the time of draft registration, preparations can be made so that an adequate claim can be made when that time comes. It is certainly best to do as much in advance as possible to have thought out the claim, made preliminary drafts of statements of belief that would have to be submitted, and to work on various ways to authenticate the claim.

Only at the last moment, after the declaration of a national emergency or emergency or war, would inductions be resumed under power granted to the president by amending the Selective Service Act. Then induction orders would be sent first to those who will be twenty years old in the current calendar year, beginning with those whose numbers are lowest (determined by lottery). The induction orders will be sent by mailgram and will instruct the potential inductees to obtain an *Information for Registrants* booklet from the post office and to return Form 9, which is also available at the post office, if they wish to be reclassified from 1-A. The *Information for Registrants* booklet explains (all too briefly) the possible classifications. Submission of Form 9 (within the time limit, as little as ten days) automatically postpones induction into the Army until the claim can be decided.

(We expect that this "emergency only" call-up procedure will be modified later in the decade of the 1980s to allow for a "peacetime" draft. Such a draft procedure would have limited call-ups, and include classification and examination of registrants prior to the issuance of induction orders. Check with knowledgeable people about this possible change; it will be widely publicized at the time.)

Making the CO Claim

The conscientious objector form, "Claim Documentation Form—Conscientious Objector," may be the best CO form that has been available. Its earlier versions were criticized by the organizations that support COs, and the result is a much improved form.

In order to properly make a claim and also to satisfy the expectations of the Selective Service System, the CO will have to keep in mind many things that are not specified by the information and instructions provided and at the same time carefully comply with the required procedure by Selective Service. If proper care is exercised, there should be little chance that a legitimate claim will be denied, though in some cases appeals may have to be made from improper decisions by the Selective Service claims board.

Three things should be kept in mind in making the claim: (1)

the general context of how Selective Service will decide about the claim, (2) the proper elements of a CO claim as the courts have decided the matter, and (3) the special problems of filling out Form 22 as it has been proposed (keeping in mind that it will be revised).

The Context of the Selective Service Decisions on CO Claims

Each registrant who makes a CO claim will have a mandatory appearance before the local Selective Service claims board. The local claims board is made up of three or more citizens who have been recruited by Selective Service personnel (almost always reservists or National Guard officers), approved by the governor (a routine review at best), and officially appointed by the president (but actually without review by the president, a *pro forma* appointment). The local claims board will tend to be motivated by patriotism and sympathy with the military, since it serves voluntarily and was recruited by military officers who tend to use their own channels for finding willing volunteers.

The boards usually will have one woman member (and no more) and racial/ethnic membership somewhat reflective of the local community. The boards will have been through a training program which simulated their operations. The boards will not have responsibilities for deciding all claims and determining who will be ordered to be drafted (which used to be the case). Only the classifications that require the exercise of judgment to determine whether or not the evidence is sufficient to grant the deferment or exemption or CO classification are subject to their review. They will consider hardship and ministerial classifications in addition to CO claims. (They will also handle appeals of denials of certain administrative classifications made by area office personnel.)

The local claims boards will employ trained military personnel instead of the previous practice of having civilian local board clerks (they were usually female and drawn from the community itself.) Since these reservists and National Guardsmen are unfamiliar with COs and understandably have a very different point of view, it is unlikely that they will be sympathetic and supportive.

The training of the local boards, while stressing fairness, has been seriously prejudiced by a design and materials that emphasize how to reject CO claimants rather than how to facilitate COs' best expression and documentation of their belief so that they would qualify. (Even as new forms and procedures are developed it will be hard to undo the impressions made in the original training.)

The circumstances in which the claim will be made and processed are not favorable to a calm and dispassionate assessment of its merits. Congress will have declared a National Emergency or even war, and restored the power to induct draftees to the president. Those involved in the Selective Service System will tend to be overwhelmingly supportive of the war preparations, and those who oppose the measures (conscientious objectors, certainly) would be seen as adversaries, even branded as traitors by some. The local claims boards will have to act quickly to determine the merits of CO claims (80,000 draftees will be inducted in the first month), for invalid CO claims delayed too long would cause some registrants to be inducted prematurely when the rejected CO claimant should have gone instead. Local claims boards could feel under pressure to decide many cases at a single sitting, giving insufficient time and attention to their merits.

Thus the circumstances, the orientation of the local board to its task, the staffing, and the form itself are prejudicial to the CO claimant. None of these factors should be so influential, however, that a properly made claim should be rejected, though in some cases it might have to be taken to court, eventually. (The case law for COs is now so well established that a properly argued, *bona fide* case can be expected to be favorably adjudicated.)

The Elements of a Valid CO Claim

In order to qualify as a CO in the U.S. conscription system, you must (1) state that you are a CO (as the law has defined it), (2) demonstrate that it is based on "religious training and belief" (as the Supreme Court has broadly defined it), and (3) that you are sincere (*Clay* v. *United States*, 1971). Over the last two decades these criteria have been established in a series of court decisions which will bind Selective Service in its administration of the CO classification process. Unfortunately, the independent organizations that assist COs (the National Interreligious Service Board for Conscientious Objectors [NISBCO] and CCCO, a national draft and military counseling agency) understand the implications of these cases in ways that are often diametrically oppposed to the interpretation the current top administrators of the Selective Service System have.

(The elements of a CO claim are expressed in the worksheet for COs which NISBCO provides, "What Do I Believe About War," which is designed as an aid to formulating the answers to the three requirements for a claim. It has a duplicate page to be filed with the appropriate religious or counseling agency the claimant wants to rely upon for advice and authentication of his claim. Both NISBCO and CCCO [which was founded as the Central Committee for Conscientious Objectors] will assist a CO in perfecting his answers and provide extensive literature as background.)

Stating your belief. You should be able to write in your own words your conscientious objection to war. The statute requires that you be "opposed to participation in war in any form." The issue is participation. There are some COs who would acknowledge that the civil authority has a right to conduct war, but they cannot conscientiously participate. They may even sympathize with the wars that other nations wage, but as Americans, cannot join in those conflicts.

Jewish applicants for CO status should be wary of getting into issues of the justifiability of wars by the State of Israel. Many people assume that Jews are automatically in favor of war because they also assume that all Jews favor without question the existence of the State of Israel and *ipso facto* its war policies, and would participate if given the opportunity. You should have thought through your answer, however, for you may be questioned at your personal appearance about your readiness to fight in Israel's wars.

The law used to be stated in terms of opposition to "all

wars," but since wars that are hypothetical for an individual or beyond the usual authority for war making have been excluded by court decisions, the present statute focuses on "participation in war in any form." What your parents did and what your God might require you to do, should there be a divine intervention from outside ordinary history, are not appropriate considerations. If you had been alive to cope with Hitler's despotism, you wouldn't be you. So, *participation* is the relevant criterion to define your relation to war. What are you willing to do personally about fighting in a real war?

"War," not just any fighting or unpremeditated violence, is what you must object to. War as an organized activity for political change is the cause to which you would be conscripted. The use of police forces, your own willingness to use force, what you would do if attacked, and whether or not you would defend another person, while important questions, *are not in question* as you seek CO status. Some board members may have these questions in mind and press you to declare yourself. Ordinary courtesy should prompt you to give honest answers, and so you will want to think out what you would do in instances that do not involve the mass actions of governments in going to war. Focus your written statement, however, on "war in any form."

"In any form" has been decided by the Supreme Court to exclude those who would choose which war they would serve in. The law excludes those who are so-called selective objectors. Some followers of traditional moral teaching about the conditions under which a war can be begun and carried out would certainly be excluded. These are the persons who think there are wars that ought to be fought in the future, and in which they would be willing to join. There are others, however, who, convinced by "justifiable war" doctrines, and the principles of "customary" international law, cannot project circumstances in which modern war will meet these tests of moral acceptability. There are some conscientious people who do not think of themselves as pacifists but who might qualify as COs by using carefully argued statements. Their cases will be harder to decide by unsophisticated local claims boards; but if that is what a registrant sincerely believes, the claim should be prepared and entered that way.

There are some registrants whose claims more likely fit into the scope of legally unacceptable "selective objector" arguments. If a person genuinely believes a particular war to be unconscionable, though not believing himself to be opposed to war in any form, a claim might be prepared primarily for the sake of vindicating his conscience. Such a claim, even though failing with the appeals process in the Selective Service System and losing in the court case that would follow, would be the basis for mitigating the sentence given. In several court cases during the Vietnam era and in some instances of noncooperation since 1980, the courts have reduced sentences to court-supervised community service or other less punitive consequences than the five years and $10,000 which could be assessed for violating the Military Selective Service Act. If a CO elects this way of expressing his conscience, the assistance of a qualified attorney would be required.

The second test of a CO claim is that one must be opposed by reason of "religious training and belief." This requirement has been defined by the Supreme Court to eliminate any favoritism toward a particular religion. In keeping with the widely held view of the Founding Fathers of the nation that the inner seat of externally observed religion is the conscience, the court has essentially affirmed conscientious belief as "religious training and belief." The legislative history of the phrase does not allow the phrase to be pulled apart into the separate components of "training" and "belief."

What you must demonstrate is that your beliefs are moral or ethical or religious, or some combination. This continuity includes some beliefs that most people would think were primarily moral principles all the way to religious commandments that seem essentially religious. If these beliefs are "so deeply held that they will give no rest or peace to be any part of an instrument of war," they qualify. The Supreme Court said in

Welsh v. *Tarr* in 1940 that Welsh qualified though he crossed out the word "religious" in the definition given on the form he used. He qualified, just as did Seeger, who, five years before, the Court judged to be qualified though he did not "believe in a Supreme Being" (*United States* v. *Seeger*, 1965). At that time Congress had added a requirement that one had to believe in a Supreme Being, and the Supreme Court threw out that limitation of the meaning of "religion." Seeger satisfied the test: "A sincere and meaningful belief which occupies in the life of its possessor a place parallel to that filled by the God of those admittedly qualifying for the exemption comes within the statutory definition" (*United States* v. *Seeger*, 1965). For the purpose of qualifying, then, there is no real distinction between moral or ethical and religious beliefs.

Your belief must not be based essentially on political, sociological, or economic considerations. It is quite all right to take these factors into account, but they cannot be the basis of the claim.

Your opposition cannot be a "merely personal moral code." The Supreme Court has defined that narrowly to exclude expediency or getting out of the draft for your own convenience. Your belief, to qualify, must be about something more important than your survival alone, and should be related to a Supreme Being in the broad sense of highest values or, of course, a traditional religious belief.

How you would express your beliefs to a draft board is covered in the section below about "Filling Out Form 22." There is a big difference between figuring out what you believe and telling others about it so they can understand you.

Demonstrating sincerity, the third criterion, is important. It is another way of showing that your belief is really a religion with you. The fact that you really believe what you claim to believe is not so easy to show. Unlike all the other classifications given by Selective Service, this one does not depend upon a set of documents or relationships that can be proved by someone else. Your beliefs are part of you and exist inside you.

They can be demonstrated by what you write and say, through the testimonies of others in person and by letter, and through consistent actions and utterances that imply your beliefs about not participating in war. You are trying to show that you are sincerely unwilling to do something. In practice, however, virtually every CO has a history of actions and statements that can be put together to make a convincing case for sincerity.

We all wish we could be consistent all the time. Showing that you live a life consistent with the belief system that includes your unwillingness to take the life of others in war would involve showing where that sort of conviction shows in your involvement in peace activities, organizations, and work for related matters of justice. What choices did you make about classes, jobs, and interests? You should point out in the sources for your belief, which you would cite in showing the moral/ethical/religious character of your belief, where you have agreement, and where these have affected your life. Just because a person has gotten angry and fought back, or for a while pursued an inconsistent activity, should not of itself disqualify. The local claims board should recognize that you are human.

Keeping a record of what you have done for peace and nonviolence will help to demonstrate sincerity. Keep papers you wrote for school, clippings of activities like a "walk for hunger" or attendance at meetings, rallies, and religious observances. If you have become a member of a formally organized group for peace, such as the Jewish Peace Fellowship, New Jewish Agenda, American Friends of Peace Now, etc., whose purposes are compatible with being a CO, by all means keep those records. Showing that other members of your family have these beliefs, too, or that significant persons in your life have helped you form your beliefs, will make your case for sincerity more convincing.

Arranging for letters of support and eventual testimony on your behalf when you have your hearing will be valuable for convincing the local board. Some people are relatively inarticulate when put on their own before authority figures such as the local Selective Service board. Having these secondary proofs of your belief will be essential for some people and a real help for all COs in making their claims.

Filling Out Form 22, and Making the Claim When the Time Comes

Form 22, "Claim Documentation Form—Conscientious Objector," will be sent to you when you submit Form 9 in response to receiving a mailgram ordering you to induction into the Army. You will have as little as ten days to report for induction, and Form 9 must be submitted by the day before induction in order to postpone the induction order. Form 9 will notify Selective Service of your request to be reclassified and allow you to specify which of the classifications you think you are eligible for. Basic information about those classifications will be provided in the *Information for Registrants* booklet which will be available at local post offices.

The Selective Service System is using Form 22 (as it uses similar forms for the hardship claim and for those who are training to be clergy or who are already recognized as full-time clergy) to document for the local claims board your claim to be classified as a CO. The form states what one must show to be classified as a CO, provides the option of making a claim for noncombatant service as a CO (1-A-O) or for exemption from both combatant and noncombatant service (1-O), and then asks the registrant to describe his beliefs that are the basis for his claim, to give their sources in religious training and belief, and to provide suggested documentation (to show sincerity).

Along with Form 22 the claimant should submit a full statement of belief such as would qualify him to be classified as a CO. These considerations were specified above. Such a statement, together with information to establish that it is based on religious training and belief, and that it is sincerely held, is a *prima facie* claim. That is to say: on the face of it the registrant qualifies. Selective Service is then in the position of having to disprove the claim.

If the claim is made inadequately, or orally at the mandatory personal appearance, there is no evidence in your file that you are a CO, for no recording of your hearing is permitted and no verbatim transcript allowed. Upon appeal, there would be no record to exhibit, and if it goes to court, there will be nothing on record. It would be your word and that of your witnesses at the hearing against the word of the government in court.

It is well to keep in mind the obsolete Form 22 as it was criticized by the national groups working for COs when it was obtained by NISBCO in late 1984. This form was a revision of the form used by Selective Service to train its local board members and other personnel in the processing of CO claims. Even when superseded, it will have left its impression on those who judge your claim. That form seemed to focus on distinguishing what sort of a CO you are (moral, ethical, or religious, and how religious you are). It also sought to weed out those who are selective objectors to war. The form in the context of the training for board members put too much emphasis on when you realized your belief. New training materials and experience will eventually obliterate the memory of that old form.

So, how should you fill out your statement and the form? *Carefully!*

The regulations direct that the answers should be concise, but you should be certain that your answer is sufficient! Tell your basic beliefs in your own words, being sure to include your belief about not participating in war.

Don't say things you don't really believe. At your personal appearance you will want to see to it that what you have written corresponds with what you say to the board members. Therefore, don't copy out things that are not the way you would say them, except where you want to show that your views are like those of a particular religious teaching that you quote.

Be detailed enough so that evidence that your belief is yours can be seen. In telling how you came to your belief, it is really helpful to board members, and to those who are writing letters for you or appearing on your behalf, for you to be autobiographical. All those details add up to proof of your sincerity.

If your convictions are based on a belief in God, you would

want to say enough about your faith in God to show how that sort of God makes you a CO. In a similar way, beliefs in love or compassion, or a belief in the sacredness, dignity, and inviolability of human life, or the brotherhood and sisterhood of humankind, or a duty to pursue peace, all have to be tied in with your statement to being a conscientious objector to "participation in war in any form."

Avoid antagonizing board members. Think of ways that you can say things that will be sympathetic with where they are. Remember that patriotism, usually a personal experience with the military that was good, and community service motivate them to be on the local claims board. In many instances they will have conservative religious beliefs and may be unfamiliar or even antagonistic to you. Broad generalizations about the motives of others, or derogatory comments especially, will do you little good and perhaps much harm. Impugning the intentions of those who are in the armed forces sets up a conflict, for most of them believe they are working for peace, too.

Avoid emphasis on political arguments both in your statement and later at your personal appearance. (It may overtake the impression you give and lead to rejection of your claim.) Along the same line, maintain a style in writing and in your conduct at the personal appearance which is in keeping with your peaceable intentions. (The local claims board is taught to take your "demeanor" into account.) So, don't be strident, self-righteous, or angry.

If you say that as a Jew you cannot participate in war, you must explain why. Not all Jews are conscientious objectors. (The bulk of this book is devoted to helping you think through that answer in the context of long tradition and teaching and through illustration with contemporary statements.)

If you believe in God and can state in good conscience that you must live in faithfulness with God's commandments, say so. Be sure to specify some of the *mitzvot* or divine mandates or imperatives that you feel you must obey. These may include the commandments not to kill, to love and respect all others, and to treat others as you wish to be treated yourself. Then explain how your beliefs relate to your refusal to participate in war specifically. Why is it a violation of God's commandments for you to enter the military?

At some point you should provide information as to whether or not your beliefs would allow you to serve as a noncombatant in the Army. You will have indicated in your response on Form 22 what category of service you are applying for. Being a 1-A-O involves a little more compromise in that, though the noncombatant is not trained with weapons nor allowed to use them, his work will assist the military effort. Even as a medic the practical effect of your work may be to return soldiers to battle, even at the cost of deferring treatment for the severely injured and the enemy. (*The Handbook for CO's* [see bibliography] has a whole chapter on thinking through this option, and NISBCO has a memo available separately.)

Tell the board about how you acquired your beliefs. If you were influenced by formal or informal Jewish education, tell about it. *Words of Conscience* (10th ed.), published by NISBCO, compiles the statements of religious groups, including appropriate Jewish statements concerning conscientious objection. They may remind you of past educational experiences and help you identify your beliefs. The book also reports some of the history of conscientious objection in America, and the witness of others to nonviolence.

The influence of your parents may be very important, especially if you have come to adopt their values. Tell about what kind of person they raised you to be. How did they teach you to handle conflict? Don't be vague. What behavior did they praise, what attitudes did they criticize or discourage?

Refer to the actual sources that have had an impact on you and have helped mold your beliefs. They may be people, organizations, pamphlets, articles, books, conversations, TV, lectures, courses, rabbis, teachers, youth group leaders, camp counselors, prayer services, songs, poems, artwork, photographs, movies, and plays. Describe each person, incident, or situation with enough detail to show the extent it impacted on you.

State how your beliefs are affecting your life. What sort of vocation are you contemplating? How do you intend to give your volunteer time? What sort of family do you want to establish, what sort of lifestyle to maintain, how do you intend to help others? These are all relevant questions, many of which can be included in your written claim, and all of which you should have thought about before meeting with the claims board at your personal appearance.

Negative experiences may even be relevant. If you belonged to ROTC and had a difficult time, morally and/or spiritually, describe how and tell how your experience relates to your feelings now.

If you can describe how you came to realize your CO beliefs, it would be helpful to the board members to learn about those circumstances, especially since they have been taught to expect that people would have a particular point at which they became aware. It may be that you will do better to put it in the context of awareness of your own moral and spiritual development. (Many people, of course, cannot pinpoint a time at which their convictions were "crystallized," and that presumption behind question 3 on old Form 22 is a serious flaw in Selective Service's understanding of conscientious objection.)

You have already described your beliefs and values. Now is the time to show how they apply to your day-to-day life and the moral choices you are called upon to make. Some examples might be:

You have never killed or intentionally hurt another human being or animal. You even have an aversion to killing ants, flies, or bugs.
You do not hunt or fish because you are opposed to the wanton destruction of animal life.
You are gentlemanly and sportsmanlike when you participate in sports. You and the "killer instinct" are mutually incompatible. You dislike the excessive roughness in sports like football or hockey. (It is interesting to note, however, that Mohammed Ali, who became a world heavyweight boxing champion, was recognized by the United States Supreme Court as a conscientious objector. There have been several instances of boxers and wrestlers adopting

nonviolent philosophies because they feared what they might do if they were in the military.)

You do not like to quarrel. Insulting, hurting, or embarrassing others is against your beliefs. Even harmful gossip is against your principles. (Jewish tradition likens such forms of behavior to murder.)

Perhaps you are a vegetarian or observe *kashruth*, the Jewish dietary laws.

You may have expressed your nonviolent principles in a journal, a composition, or an essay for a course; in correspondence; in a high school, college, or hometown newspaper or magazine; in a youth group periodical, temple bulletin, or Hillel publication. (Save these to show as evidence to your draft board.) You may have expressed these principles orally in a debate club speech, a talk at your temple or Hillel organization, or in a dormitory conversation.

You have participated in a peace or CO group or course. Perhaps you even started such a group. You subscribe to peace magazines. You even have a peace and nonviolence library.

Point out that you have taken the time and trouble to answer these six questions before the answers were required.

You would rather go to jail than enter the military. (State this not defiantly, but as a moral/religious scruple.)

You have been a conciliator or peacemaker.

If you cannot show concretely the depth of your antiviolence feelings, remember that this question expects you to prove the depth of your beliefs in general. Offer evidence of this by showing how you may have upheld your moral or religious beliefs in the face of a challenge or a threat.

You have gone hungry rather than eat meat or unkosher food.

You will not take exams on the Sabbath or on a holyday.

You have arranged to leave school or work early in order to celebrate the Sabbath or a holyday.

Your religious or moral beliefs have prevented your doing something that cost you a job, an honor, a membership in a group, or something else you wanted.

Thus, you should think about your life and try to connect and intertwine all the information that testifies to your nonviolence and the strength of your beliefs.

Old C. O. Form 150, in use until 1972, pursued the theme of

sincerity with specific requests for information which are instructive. (These will appear on new Form 22 [revised].) Describe how your beliefs affect the way you live, the type of
work you do or plan to do to earn a living, or the types of
activity you participate in during nonworking hours.

As a young objector you may have had little work experience, but you can show how deeply you hold your beliefs by
discussing your future plans and how they relate to nonviolence. Answering this question gives you the opportunity to
describe your future career plans. You may discuss both the
kinds of jobs you would like to have and those you would not
accept. The contrast can be dramatic and telling.

If you would never work in a defense plant, a nuclear missile
factory, or a slaughterhouse, point that out. If you would never
be a police officer, FBI agent, CIA agent, or any other law
enforcement agent, explain why, but not disrespectfully. Discuss your preferences from a religious or moral perspective,
not a political one. For example, if you attribute your opposition to working for such institutions to their role in preserving
the status quo, that would be a political statement. Many COs
talk about how they would never work in any occupation
where they would be required to inflict death or injury on
another living thing. That would certainly be a statement based
on a moral belief.

After describing what you would not do, talk about what
you intend to do and link it to your nonviolent beliefs. If you
are unsure about your career, discuss several possibilities. If
you want to be an engineer, architect, contractor, or carpenter,
you might point out that these are professions that build, not
destroy. If you plan to be a gardener or a forest ranger, contrast
the beauty of the environment and the serenity of nature with
the destructiveness and inhumanity of war. If you intend to
study music, speak of harmony. If you are studying to be a
doctor or a dentist or have considered doing medical research,
discuss the concept of healing and of extending life. If you are
going to enter government service or city planning, talk about
your commitment to improving the quality of life and the

condition of all people. With respect to the profession of law, write about protecting human rights and civil liberties, extending equal opportunity to all, and defending justice and peace. (Some time ago, I officiated at the funeral and burial of Louis Showstack, a seventy-five-year-old lawyer friend of mine who would never participate in a divorce or eviction case. He could not allow himself to be party to inflicting misery on another human being.) Such outlooks toward these professions would help your draft board understand your commitment to your principles.

Whatever kind of work you plan to do, show how your nonviolent nature interprets your feelings toward it. If you plan to enter the counseling field, describe your devotion to helping others gain mental health, personal well-being, and *shalom*, that is, wholeness. If you are headed toward a career in education, talk about the importance of an educated citizenry that is in pursuit of knowledge and truth. If you intend to become a rabbi, discuss your future role as a teacher of Jewish ideals and imperatives, especially the pursuit of peace and justice. Whatever your career plans or interests, contrast their positive features with the destructive ones of the occupations you would not undertake. This contrast will make your answer very effective.

Perhaps you already have a job that you could discuss here. Talk about how it is compatible with your nonviolent nature and in keeping with the depth of your feelings. At the least you might be able to say that in your work you are more concerned with your effect on the well-being of others than with your own personal or material gain.

Participation in antiwar activities is a good indication to your draft board of your sincerity. If you are involved in such activities, explain the nonpolitical commitments that are important to you. Tell about any activity or demonstration in which you have participated. (The more you have been in, the better.) Explain why being part of such a demonstration shows the consistency of your beliefs. (If you participate in antiwar or antidraft activities, have a picture taken of you standing next to a placard bearing a peace message like "No More Wars" or wearing a T-shirt or sweatshirt bearing a peace message. Save it for your personal hearing with your draft board.) If you write letters to newspapers on the subject of peace, mention them here and save them to show at your hearing as well. Such evidence of your peace activities will tell your board much about you.

In general, you should also describe your lifestyle. Cite your life's goals and discuss how they have grown out of your beliefs. Don't confine your response to your beliefs on war alone. This is your chance to demonstrate the relationship of your value system as a whole to your daily life and the moral choices you make all the time.

Portray any specific actions or incidents of your life that show you believe as you do. This gives you another chance to show proof of your sincerity as a CO. If you have ever walked away from a challenge to a fight, describe that incident here. Most men have had a similar experience during their lives. Draft board members may be able to relate to your story. Include incidents in which the moral choices you made were consistent with your beliefs and might have cost you something. Show that you were faithful to your beliefs despite the cost.

If you run out of new things to say by the time you get to the sixth question, simply refer back to your answers to the previous questions. Restate them in other words. Repetition will not hurt your claim.

A good CO claim tends to be about ten double-spaced typewritten pages at most. Given the instructions of the regulations asking you to be concise, and the likelihood that it will not be read if too long, try to see how you can shrink it without losing important information, and try to organize it so that your main points that satisfy the requirements are highlighted.

Once you have completed your first draft, share your work with a skilled draft or CO counselor. (Contact the Jewish Peace Fellowship for the names of rabbis who specialize in this subject or CO counselors in your area.) You should also show your work to your Hillel and/or congregational rabbi. Benefit from their critiques and improve your answers. Send a draft to the Central Committee for Conscientious Objectors and the National Interreligious Service Board for Conscientious Objectors, requesting evaluations from them as well.

Sign the bottom of each page of your final draft except the last page. Take the entire claim to a notary public, sign the bottom of the last page in the notary's presence, and have your signature duly notarized. Make sure to leave enough space on the last page for the notary's stamp and signature. Make several copies of the notarized document. You will want to file these with your Hillel director, with the others mentioned above, and with the various CO organizations. You will also need copies to show to those people from whom you will be requesting letters of support. (More on this below.)

This draft is, of course, a preliminary statement of your CO beliefs at this time. When it comes time to make your formal claim, you will write it answering the questions that will be on that claim. You can see, however, the importance of working through this preliminary claim ahead of time. You will have thought a great deal about your beliefs, and they will have become crystallized in your mind. You will have shown your long-standing feelings of conscientious objection by writing this preliminary claim and filing it with the various CO organizations. If your beliefs have not changed significantly by the time you write your formal claim, you may bring this notarized one with you to your draft board hearing. It will serve as an exhibit in testimony to your long-held beliefs. If, on the other hand, your ideas and beliefs have changed significantly by the time you must write your formal claim, do not confuse your draft board by submitting this evidence of your old ideas. It is important to emphasize again, though, that the time element will be very constricting when you are forced to make your claim. Having written your preliminary draft will help make the final one easier to write.

Latest Developments on the CO Form: An Update

As of this writing (1985), the Selective Service System appears intent upon altering radically CO Form 150, which was in use when inductions came to a halt in 1972. In its place, S.S. Form

22, described below may ultimately emerge as the new "Claim Documentation Form [for] Conscientious Objector."

Earlier in this chapter, I have retained the questions posed by Form 150, along with the discussion they elicit, for a variety of reasons. To begin with, they will surely be of more than casual historical and philosophic interest to any serious theorist and/ or practitioner of Jewish nonviolence. Secondly, although the proposed S.S. Form 22 will differ markedly from its predecessor if it becomes a reality, much of the discussion of Form 150 will remain substantively relevant to Form 22 and, especially, the task of composing an accompanying statement for it. Finally, the proposed Form 22 contains so many problems, inconsistencies, and ensnarements that it is being seriously contested by the National Interreligious Service Board for Conscientious Objectors and the Central Committee for Conscientious Objectors, among others. Their objections are so cogent and their opposition so forceful that Form 22 may ultimately be relegated to oblivion. Even if that happy prospect fails to materialize and Form 22 comes to see the light of day, its existence may turn out to be short-lived through eventual court action.

Be that as it may, for now we must anticipate the emergence of Form 22 for conscientious objectors. Accurately and less than affectionately dubbed "Catch 22" by its critics, for reasons which will be self-evident, Form 22 is subdivided into three sections. Part I poses six questions which we will present momentarily; Part II tells the claimant to "List below all letters and documents which you are submitting with this form"; Part III consists of a "Registrant Certification," requiring the date and the signature of the registrant attesting to the statement, "I certify that all of the information I have provided in this form and upon other documents that I am submitting to support this claim are true, accurate, and complete to the best of my knowledge and belief." We return, then, to the six questions of Part I.

    1. a. Is your objection to participation in war in any form based on religious training and belief?   Yes ☐   No ☐

    b. Is your opposition to participation in war in any form based on religious tenets or teachings?   Yes ☐ No ☐

2. Is your objection to participation in war in any form based on moral or ethical beliefs?   Yes ☐ No ☐

3. Explain the circumstances under which you first realized that you were opposed to participation in war in any form and the approximate date of your realization.

4. Are you opposed to participation in all wars?   Yes ☐ No ☐

5. Are there conditions under which your belief would permit you to participate in a particular war?   Yes ☐ No ☐

6. Check the box in front of the statement below which applies to your claim.

    ☐ I claim exemption only from training and service as a combatant member of the Armed Forces (Class 1-A-O).

    ☐ I claim exemption from any training and service as a member of the Armed Forces (Class 1-O).

Some of the questions represent devious rewordings of Form 150. Much of the previous information, therefore, remains relevant. It is of the utmost importance not to be misled. Read the questions very deliberately and formulate your answers carefully. Do not feel constrained to limit your answers to the space provided; it is clearly inadequate. Do not allow yourself to be unnecessarily confused by a form which is calculated to confound. For example, question 1 asks for your religious beliefs (take the word "tenets," altogether superfluous though it is, as a synonym for "beliefs") and training, while question 2 focuses on "moral or ethical beliefs." Do not infer that, according to the law, moral or ethical beliefs are inferior to religious ones insofar as validity for CO status is concerned. That is not the case, and you may have to impress that upon your draft board. Remember, and if necessary stress to your board, that by law orthodox and unorthodox believers alike qualify for CO status (Supreme Court, *Seeger*, 1965), and that the law recognizes moral/ethical beliefs on precisely the same par as religious ones when either are "so deeply held as to give no rest nor peace" (Supreme Court, *Welsh*, 1970). One is as qualifying as the other. The phraseology of the *United States* v. *Seeger* Supreme Court decision (1965) is especially enlightening in this regard. It spoke of a religious belief as a "sincere and meaningful" belief . . . that "occupies a place in the life of its possessor parallel to that filled by [an] orthodox belief in God."

The impertinent question 3, commonly known as the issue of "crystallization," could pose problems for some. Longtime COs, for example, especially applicants who grew up from their early years on nonviolence, may have a hard time pinpointing when they first realized their beliefs. If this question survives, handle it as precisely as you can, offering as extensive a history as possible. In the past, this question was once used to disqualify applicants who had arrived at their CO commitments late in the game. Under the new system that is now in place, the "approximate date of realization" is irrelevant, since all COs will be submitting their claims upon receiving an induction notice. There is no longer a provision for applying early or ahead of time as a CO to the Selective Service System.

Question 4 departs elusively from the earlier terminology of questions 1–3, namely, "war in any form," in favor of the tricky phrase "in all wars." Beware. The phrase "in all wars" has been outmoded for some twenty-five years. The law requires opposition to participating in "war in any form," which differs from "all wars." The CO claimant is required to express and substantiate religious and/or moral/ethical objections to participating in "war in any form," as limited to cases of *real* war, under secular, temporal authority, in the present and likely future, not wars in the distant past (before the claimants were even born) and not contrived, hypothetical, future wars. In reality, this question is actually a set-up for the next question. Clearly, checking the "no" box here will lead to disqualification.

Question 5, a reformulation of the preceding question, is the real trap. Any claimant who innocently falls into the pitfall of checking the "yes" box will immediately appear as a selective

objector and will be a surefire candidate for automatic disqualification. There are, no doubt, some religious COs who, on
theological grounds, would participate in some way in a divinely commanded war. This is not pertinent to a CO claim but
might lead to a disqualifying "yes" answer. Alternatively,
believers in the "just war" doctrine may now consider that to
be an impossibility in the face of the potential for nuclear war,
but would participate in a "just war" if it were to exist. This,
too, would disqualify the claimant. Be careful lest you get
unsuspectingly ensnared, only to lose your claim.

Conspicuously missing in Form 22 are the questions about
lifestyle through which Form 150 allowed the claimant to
demonstrate his sincerity. Though it is obviously not geared to
this purpose, question 3 could be interpreted so as to allow you
to weave the lifestyle issue into your answer.

Remember the straightforward definition of the CO and
share it with as many of your peers as possible. Unlike Form
150, Form 22 unfortunately omits the definition of the CO. The
definition that recommends itself is that of the Supreme Court,
which outlined the basic criteria for conscientious objection in
Clay v. *United States* (1971). These define the CO as one who (1)
is "religious" according to the Supreme Court's definition
(which includes the moral/ethical and the unorthodox religious
belief), (2) objects to war in any form, and (3) is sincere in his
claim.

A Postscript

As this book goes off to the printer in the summer of 1985, the
Selective Service System has begun to manifest flexibility in
connection with Form 22 as described in this chapter. Recog-
nizing its abundant defects, the System is at work improving it.
The most recent, unpublished draft of Form 22 in its newest
revision will clearly state the legal definition of a C. O. and it
will apparently allow the claimant to append a statement or
essay of his own. In general it is comparable to the old Form
150. Hopefully, that reasonable trend will prevail. However, it
is still only a "draft" form. What will finally emerge is anyone's
guess at this point.

Declarations on Conscientious Objection by Jewish Organizations

Before, during, and after you have written your rough draft, continue to read as much of the literature on conscientious objection as you can. (The bibliography later in this work will give you a good start.) In forming your own conscientious objector ideas, in writing your answers to the CO claim questions, and in preparing for your hearing with the draft board, you should continue to think about the Jewish ideals that have, no doubt, influenced your life. These are ideals such as the sanctity and inviolability of life; reverence for all the living and for the dead as well; the sacredness of all creation; the centrality of love, compassion, caring, mercy, and fellow-feeling; the sinfulness of bloodshed; the abhorrence of violence, both individual and collective; the pursuit of social justice and righteousness; the concern for humankind (including the enemy); the emphasis on reason and rationality; and the commonality of humanity. Jewish ideals also include compassion for animals, the responsibility for maintaining the beauty and integrity of nature, the stress on truth, the importance of the family unit, the vision of peace and the responsibility for all to strive for it, and the concept of one's absolute responsibility to God, who is the Ultimate, Absolute Authority.

Dwell on these and other pertinent Jewish teachings and values that have had an impact on your life as you think about and discuss your CO beliefs. Then go on to complete the picture by integrating your Jewish values with your more personal values. You want your draft board to know that you are a loyal Jew, standing firmly on the eternal ground of tradition, and a sensitive, thoughtful individual who is grappling with questions that are both timeless and timely: the moral and ethical issues of human decency, conscience, and moral judgment. This is the best possible combination of ideas and ideals for your claim.

The following are relevant declarations by various official Jewish organizations on the subject of conscientious objection. Use them in your essays or just think about them.

From the Central Conference of American Rabbis, the international association of Reform rabbis:

> Conscientious objection to military service is in accordance with the highest interpretation of Judaism.

From the Rabbinical Assembly of America, the association of Conservative rabbis:

> We recognize the right of the Conscientious Objector to claim exemption from military service in any war in which he cannot give his moral assent, and we pledge ourselves to support him in his determination to refrain from any participation in it.

From "Enlighten Our Conscience," a religious statement on registration for the draft that was issued on July 20, 1980, by a coalition of religious and peace groups and signed by rabbinic leaders of the Union of American Hebrew Congregations' Social Action Center, the Southern California Board of Rabbis, and the Central Conference of American Rabbis:

> As national religious leaders, we call upon all Americans, especially upon those in positions of power, to reflect upon whether true national security can be accomplished through preparation for war or rather through God's command to act justly. We urge all American young people to consider seriously the moral implications of registration for the military draft. We pledge our pastoral support to those who choose nonregistration for rea-

sons of conscience. We urge young Americans to consider conscientious objector status should the draft be reinstituted . . . Those who choose to serve in the military should be mindful of the moral implications of the use of indiscriminate weaponry which our country stands ready to use against every woman, man and child in an adversary nation.

During these dark times may the God of truth enlighten our consciences to do the works that make for peace.

The essential belief of the Jewish Peace Fellowship:

The J.P.F. is an interdenominational, international Jewish organization that supports conscientious objectors and maintains that nonviolence and conscientious objection stem directly from the loftiest mandates and teachings of Judaism. The Fellowship unites those who believe that Jewish ideals and experience provide inspiration for a nonviolent commitment to life and the remaking of society.

The role of the Synagogue Council of America:

The council is an umbrella organization embracing the rabbinical and synagogal bodies of Orthodoxy, Reform, and Conservatism. It recognizes the place of Jewish conscientious objection by its membership in the National Interreligious Service Board for Conscientious Objectors.

The statement of the Reconstructionist Rabbinical Association, published in the *Reconstructionist*, vol. 47 (April 1981):

The Jewish people have historically placed great value on peace. Judaism identifies *Shalom* (Peace) as a Divine Name. (Vayikra Rabba 9:9)

The responsibility to "seek peace and pursue it" (Ps. 34:15) extends even to those tragic situations where war seems inevitable. Maimonides, in the twelfth century, wrote "you are prohibited from waging war against anyone in the world until you have attempted a peaceful solution to the problem." (Mishnch Torah, Laws of Kings 6:1) In this period of increased international tensions, the need for seeking peaceful solutions is paramount.

We see this obligation to seek peace as incumbent on all people of good will. Warfare and violence diminish our common humanity and our share in the divine image. Peace should be pursued among nations, within our country, within our communities, and within our families.

Judaism is not monolithic in its approach to carrying out the obligation of peace. It acknowledges that there may be various answers to particular moral dilemmas.

The Reconstructionist Rabbinical Association recognizes that many Jews will find in our tradition and experience sanction for participation in military service. But we also recognize that many Jews will find that they cannot endorse or participate in military service. We recognize the right of men and women, basing themselves in the Jewish tradition, to take a position of conscience against participation in warfare. This may be either as Conscientious Objectors or as Selective Conscientious Objectors to a specific war or types of wars.

We therefore urge the Government of the United States to uphold the rights of those who are Conscientious Objectors to any war and of Selective Conscientious Objectors to specific wars or types of wars.

We urge our members, congregations, and communities to make information on the draft, including the nature of CO status, available to young people now that registration has been reinstated.

Finally, we urge that a spirit of seeking peace unite those who may actually face the difficult decisions regarding military service or Conscientious Objection. Neither position can be an end in itself.

The Reconstructionist Rabbinical Association will support the needs of those who are compelled to take a moral stand against military conscription. We will support efforts to discuss war and peace, to increase understanding among conflicting groups, and to reduce the threats of warfare and nuclear annihilation.

A resolution adopted at the ninety-third annual convention of the Central Conference of American Rabbis, June 28 to July 1, 1982:

Whereas we have previously recognized the right of both conscientious objection and selective conscientious objection to war; and

Whereas registration at this time is unnecessary; and

Whereas, believing that the costs of such an action draw funds from needed social, educational, and economic programs that will make for social betterment,

Resolved, that the Central Conference of American Rabbis opposes the inauguration or implementation by our government of any national draft at this time. Similarly, we oppose the ideas of registering our youth at this time for some future draft. We believe that should there arise some national emergency necessitating the mobilization of our population, sufficient techniques exist by which to effect that mobilization.

Further resolved, that we urge our colleagues to provide counseling services to interested and affected individuals, and to advertise widely this service in and through the community, so that Jewish youth particularly might know where they might go for counseling that is based on the Jewish religious tradition.

Reread some of the general literature of nonviolence and strengthen your acquaintance with its greats. Among those you should be sure to look at are the biblical prophets, Gandhi, Martin Luther King, Jr., Martin Buber, Judah Magnes, Dorothy Day, Henry David Thoreau, Leo Tolstoy, A. J. Muste, Pope John XXIII, and Cesar Chavez. Quote from any of the above statements and include the teachings of the great thinkers on nonviolence wherever they are relevant to your own ideas. They will add focus and integrity to your own thoughts and written beliefs.

One final point ought to be included here. In advising a young man on how to write a CO claim, a counselor always has to make a difficult decision: Whether to advise him to conform to the law as the Selective Service understands it or as the courts may interpret it. Since the Selective Service sometimes misinterprets the law, it is best for a counselor to know what the courts have said and to help a young man write a claim that meets the courts' standards. Get a good draft counselor or attorney to help you write your claim or check it afterwards. There is too much work involved and too much at stake to do an inappropriate job.

Letters of Support

Letters of support are very important in the process of your conscientious objector claim. They are, perhaps, even as vital as your CO essay. Draft boards have been known to base their judgments on the strength of these support letters. It would be hard to accuse a CO of insincerity in the face of letters to the contrary from respected people.

Start collecting your letters from the beginning. The people you are counting on may be unavailable when you need their letters later on. Or they may be unable to do a thoughtful, helpful job of writing on short notice should your claim come suddenly due.

Give much thought and care to your selection of references. They should be people who know you well, are familiar with the position you are taking, and can attest with certainty to your sincerity.

Try for a good cross section of people. You will need no more than five or six good letters. (Two or three should be solicited now, and two or three should be dated closer to the time when you make your formal claim as a conscientious objector.) Don't overlook the people who know you best of all—your parents, your girlfriend, your closest personal friend. Think of your rabbi, school teachers or administrators, coaches, parents of friends, advisers, scout leaders, camp directors or counselors, classmates, roommates, or relatives. Ask your fellow workers or employers. Consider your doctor, dentist, orthodontist, piano teacher, or family lawyer. Don't feel that someone is too close to you, overly biased in your favor, or not important enough in the opinion of your draft board to give you a good reference.

If you are in therapy, your psychotherapist would be an excellent reference for you. This is a complex issue, however. Sometimes a CO who is in therapy can qualify for a 4-F classification as well as CO status. (It is possible to apply for more than one classification at a time.) The therapist may then provide two letters for you, one for CO status, the other for disqualification on mental grounds. At this writing adequate provision has not been made for reclassification as 4-F in advance of the actual order to induction when the determination would be made by doctors at the military examination and processing station (formerly called "induction station"). Surely, by the time the draft regulations are revised in 1985 this problem will be handled more adequately.

You will probably be permitted to be classified 4-F by submitting proper information to your local Selective Service area office, and these letters from your doctor will either suffice or Selective Service will order you to a preinduction physical at the the old induction center, or what is known as the "Military Entrance and Processing Station" ("MEPS") itself. The written standards for examination are available from draft counseling groups. You will want to be careful not to let a letter describing mental health problems conflict with the documentation about being a CO. Here's where a good counselor should give advice as to how to proceed.

Those who are very close to you should be able to testify to the strength and depth of your beliefs as a conscientious objector. Some may be able to say that over the years they have watched you evolve into a nonviolent human being. Others, such as older friends, teachers, past acquaintances, or even someone like your pediatrician, may be able to confirm that your nonviolent beliefs are long held. Don't hesitate to ask these people for letters of support even though you are no longer in close touch with them.

It is not essential that your references themselves agree with your beliefs. Not at all. As a matter of fact, the letters that are potentially of the most assistance are frequently contributed by individuals who disagree with the CO position. They may express that disagreement outspokenly in their letters but will go on to describe your sincerity and the strength and depth of your convictions. The authors of such letters (including parents) are often military veterans themselves. They should not hesitate to point with pride to their own military records or experiences. Such letters of support would be very valuable to your claim.

You should also try to get one general character recommendation from the most distinguished person you can find. This could be helpful even if that person does not know you too well.

Give each person who is to write a letter for you a statement of your position as a conscientious objector. A copy of your CO essay would do very well. Explain to them what a conscientious objector is and why it is necessary for you to be readying your claim now, when there isn't even a draft. You might want to include some pamphlets from NISBCO and CCCO. *Who Is a C.O.?* from NISBCO is an especially good one. Explain fully the five questions that they should answer, which are included below. And stress that the best letters are those that are detailed, personal, and specific.

Ask each person to type or write each letter very legibly, to include his or her full name and address, to address it "To Whom It May Concern," and to make sure it is properly dated. Suggest that the letter be about one page long.

Here are five questions that should be answered in a good letter of support for a conscientious objector claim.

1. What is your relationship to the claimant and how long have you known him?
2. Do you believe that the applicant is sincere in his CO claim? On what basis?
3. To the best of your knowledge, has the applicant's conduct since arriving at this belief been consistent with this claim? Offer specific evidence.

4. Do you believe that the applicant's claim is based on deeply held religious, moral, and/or ethical beliefs, however broadly defined? How so? Wherever possible offer examples of pertinent religious and moral beliefs that you know the claimant holds. Also, offer examples of influence or training in the claimant's life, from early youth on, that you feel might have led to the development and realization of his conscientious objector position.

5. As a citizen do you have reservations of your own as to the rightness of the CO position? If you have reservations or disagreements, express them candidly and clearly. If you are a military veteran, in whatever capacity, if you are a member of the Jewish War Veterans and/or any other veterans' group, don't hesitate to mention it. This is especially necessary if your military background is the reason for your reservation or disagreement with the CO position. Naturally, if you have received any award or other positive recognition for distinguished and/or lengthy military service, make reference to it.

You, the claimant, must be sure to read each letter carefully. Eliminate any letter that is vague, too general, or inaccurate. Eliminate those that do not answer the questions listed above. Make sure no statements contradict anything you have said in your CO essay. (For example, someone might say that you eat meat, but you have said you are a vegetarian.) Such letters would hurt your claim and should not be included.

File these letters of support with your preliminary CO essay draft. You may want to add to them as time goes by. You will also want to include in this file any letters to editors, term papers, speeches, or other relevant and potentially helpful materials that reflect your CO beliefs. Keep this file up to date so that you will be ready to submit your claim on very short notice.

Late Conscientious Objectors

If you have not attended to all this ahead of time and are faced with an impending draft or, worse still, an induction notice, don't despair. The time may be short, but you may still be able to put together a CO claim and collect the necessary letters. Under the pressure of registration, perhaps you have just come to realize that you are a truly nonviolent person and could not possibly fight in a war or even be in the military. Under the pressure of time, the liability of your late awareness of being a CO may possibly be converted into an advantage by a persuasive letter of support. One such letter some years ago concluded with the following paragraphs:

> It is obviously rather late for Mr. Smith to be applying for 1-0 status. The lateness of his application may lead you to suspect that he is insincere; that he is merely exercising this option in order to evade military service. This is not the case. Rather, he applies so late because the position of conscientious objection did not come to him easily or quickly. It was a long, gradual process, involving deep and extensive soul-searching. He, for his part, in being honest and aboveboard, could not in good conscience apply earlier, while he still had doubts, even though this would have been to his advantage. I hope you will give credence to this statement, because I know it to be true.
>
> It is my fervent hope, gentlemen, that you will act affirmatively on Mr. Smith's application and grant him status 1-0. He is not seeking to evade responsibility. He is loyal to his country. He is more than willing to serve his country and society in the cause of peace, in the public good, outside the framework of the armed forces. Please give him this opportunity.

Joining or Starting Peace Groups

Once you have prepared your preliminary conscientious objector essay and have gathered some support letters (hopefully all this has been done early), you should become more active in the peace movement. It is time for you to join several peace groups or even to start your own. Do this even if you are a nonjoiner. The dues and subscription rates you will have to pay are modest. (Most have discounted rates for students.) These organizations deserve your support. Your commitment to nonviolence will be deepened through your activities with them. And memberships in peace organizations are yet more evidence in support of your CO claim.

Recommended Groups

Several of these worthwhile groups are not truly membership organizations. They do, however, send out valuable materials and have moderate rates for mailings. Instead of entering subscriptions with them, a person asks to be placed on their mailing lists. (Two such organizations are the CCCO and NISBCO, which are listed among others below.) You will find their materials interesting and invaluable.

Jewish Peace Fellowship (JPF): P.O. Box 271, Nyack, NY 10960.

The only national Jewish peace organization, JPF publishes helpful materials, such as its quarterly newsletter, *Shalom: The Jewish Peace Letter*, and it has a CO register. As a member of JPF you will be eligible to participate in the nomination of candidates for the annual Abraham Joshua Heschel Peace Award, presented for the first time in 1984 to Seymour Melman (national co-chair of SANE Nuclear Policy).

National Interreligious Service Board for Conscientious Objectors (NISBCO): 800 Eighteenth Street, N.W., Suite 600; Washington, DC 20006 (Phone 202-293-5962).

NISBCO is a must resource. Those who request assistance with their form can ask to be put on the mailing list. NISBCO provides a work sheet, "What Do I Believe About War?", the reference book *Words of Conscience* @$5, a monthly newsletter *The Reporter for Conscience Sake* @$10, and other literature, including a draft counselor's manual based on working with the regulations and administrative procedures ($15 plus $5 annual updating service). Its staff evaluates drafts of CO claims by correspondence. In the context of inductions, NISBCO specializes in negotiating alternative service opportunities.

CCCO, a draft and military counseling agency (founded as the Central Committee for Conscientious Objectors): 2208 South Street, Philadelphia, PA 19146 (Phone 215-545-4626); CCCO-West: 1215 Second Avenue, San Francisco, CA 94122 (Phone 415-566-0500).

CCCO sends out *News Notes* free to its supporters and to COs who register with it. It is another "must" mailing list to be on. It is in touch with draft counselors in every area. Its publications include the *Handbook for Conscientious Objectors*, also known as the "CO Handbook"; the twelfth edition is now slightly out of date but still indispensable. The *Objector* is a newsletter giving information of interest primarily to draft and military counselors, and the CCCO draft counselors' manual is helpful in its thematic approach. CCCO also evaluates CO claims, and has an extensive literature list. CCCO has a traveling field staff member and also gives assistance to all sorts of cases of people in the military who want to get out.

A Separate Peace (ASP): 3304 16th Street, Suite 105, San Francisco, CA 94103 (Phone 415-621-7418).

A superb draft and military counseling service, it publishes an excellent repertoire of very helpful materials.

American Friends Service Committee (AFSC): 1501 Cherry Street, Philadelphia, PA 19102 (Phone 215-241-7180).

A Quaker-sponsored peace activist group, this organization has many fine draft-counseling services in many regions and publishes useful materials.

Fellowship of Reconciliation (FOR): P.O. Box 271, Nyack, NY 10960 (Phone 914-358-4601).

This is the sponsoring group with which JPF is affiliated along with other denominational groups like the Catholic Peace Fellowship and the Episcopal Peace Fellowship. It publishes *Fellowship Magazine*, a superb resource.

American Civil Liberties Union (ACLU): 132 West 43rd Street, New York, NY 10036 (Phone 212-944-9800).

Your membership will include a subscription to the ACLU paper, *Civil Liberties*.

Amnesty International (AI): 304 West 58th Street, New York, NY 10019 (Phone 212-582-4440).

Your membership will include subscriptions to AI's *Amnesty Action* and *Matchbox*.

Center on Law and Pacifism: Mailing address: P.O. Box 1584, Colorado Springs, CO 80801; address: 233 East Fountain Boulevard, Colorado Springs, CO 80903 (Phone 303-635-0041).

Women's International League for Peace and Freedom (WILPF): 1213 Race Street, Philadelphia, PA 19107 (Phone 215-563-7110).

Women's Strike for Peace: 201 Massachusetts Avenue, N.E., Washington, DC 20002 (Phone 202-546-7397).

War Resisters League (WRL): 339 Lafayette Street, New York, NY 10012 (Phone 212-228-0450).

This is the American arm of the worldwide pacifist organization, War Resisters International (WRI). It publishes the *Non-Violent Activist*, edited by David Croteau.

New Jewish Agenda: 150 Fifth Avenue, Suite 1002, New York, NY 10011 (Phone 212-620-0828).

"Agenda," as it is called, has branches in many cities. It is a relatively new, grass-roots, national Jewish organization that defines itself as a progressive Jewish voice and organizing force on Jewish and general issues.

Magazines and Periodicals

Two Jewish periodicals with which you should become familiar for their consistently progressive and nonviolent perspectives are *Menorah*, edited by Arthur Waskow (Public Resource Center, 7041 McCallum Street, Philadelphia, PA 19119), and *Jewish Currents*, published by the Association for Promotion of Jewish Secularism (Rm. 601, 22 East 17th Street, New York, NY 10003-3272), edited by the longtime activist, Morris V. Schappes.

Other Jewish periodicals that often reflect progressive slants are *Moment, Shma, Jewish Spectator, Reform Judaism*, the *Reconstructionist, Present Tense, Jewish Frontier, Israel Horizons*, and *Genesis II* (99 Bishop Allen Drive, Cambridge, MA 02139).

In addition, I advise you to become a subscriber to or a regular reader of *New Outlook* (107 Rechov HaHashmonaim, Tel Aviv, Israel). This magazine is a peace-oriented political periodical of special interest to those concerned with Arab-Jewish rapprochement and Mideast peace. It is highly recommended for COs. A refreshing, down-under offspring of and counterpart to *New Outlook* is the Australian magazine, *Paths to Peace* (c/o Rothfield, Box 35, Fairfield 3078, Victoria, Australia).

The following are general political magazines of a peace orientation that you may want to become familiar with as a peace person: *Mother Jones*, the *Progressive*, the *Nation*, the *New Republic*, and *The New Yorker*.

The national and local groups that are dedicated specifically to the mobilization for nuclear disarmament also merit your membership and support. Foremost among these are:

Clergy and Laity Concerned (CALC): 198 Broadway, New York, NY 10038.

Interfaith Center to Reverse the Arms Race: 132 North Euclid Avenue, Pasadena, CA 91101.

Mobilization for Survival: 853 Broadway, New York, NY 10003.

Physicians for Social Responsibility (PSR): 639 Massachusetts Avenue, Cambridge, MA 02139.

Union of Concerned Scientists (USC): 1384 Massachusetts Avenue, Cambridge, MA 02138.

Educators for Social Responsibility: 639 Massachusetts Avenue, Cambridge, MA 02139.

Ground Zero, 806 15th Street, N.W., Suite 421, Washington, DC 20005.

Center for Defense Information: 303 Capitol Gallery West, 600 Maryland Avenue, S.W., Washington, DC 20024.

SANE: 711 G Street, S.W., Washington, DC 20003.

Student-Teacher Organization to Prevent Nuclear War (STOP): Box 232, Northfield, MA 01360.

Council for a Livable World: 100 Maryland Avenue, N.E., Washington, DC 20002

Facing History and Ourselves, National Foundation, Inc.: 333 Washington Street, Brookline, MA 02146.

This is an outstanding educational enterprise which has produced a superb curriculum dealing principally with the Holocaust. It treats the Holocaust as both a Jewish issue and a human, universal issue. Like the noted authors and Holocaust survivors Elie Wiesel and Samuel Pisar, among others, it attempts to apply the lessons of the Nazi Holocaust to the extraordinary danger of nuclear holocaust. It would be useful for you to become familiar with the published work of this organization, entitled *Facing History and Ourselves: Holocaust and Human Behavior,* by Margot Stern Strom and William S. Parsons (Watertown, Mass.: Intentional Educations, 1982).

In addition to the aforementioned groups, you should be aware that there are specifically Jewish organizations, both old and new, that have been dealing with the nuclear issue from a Jewish perspective. These include the following:

Religious Action Center of the Union of American Hebrew Congregations: 2027 Massachusetts Avenue, N.W., Washington, DC 20036.

This is an educational and activist Jewish resource which publishes an excellent newsletter as well as other vital materials. You should become especially familiar with its recent book, *Preventing the Nuclear Holocaust: A Jewish Response,* edited by Rabbi David Saperstein (Washington, D.C., 1983).

Another valuable book on the same subject has been published by
New York's Pilgrim Press (1982). It is *The Disarmament Catalogue,*
edited by Murray Polner. Essentially a secular book, it includes
significant Jewish elements. The *Jewish Peace Letter* (vol. 1, no. 1,
Fall 1983) describes this outstanding volume as "a treasure trove of
resources for working against the infiltration of militarism in our
culture. Besides organizations, the author gives us films, books,
peace studies' programs, museum project ideas, strategies. There
is an excellent section on rearing children. And the Jewish peace
tradition is woven throughout this book."

Shalom Center: c/o Reconstructionist Rabbinical College, Church
Road and Greenwood Avenue, Wyncote, PA 19119.

A new research and activist clearing house, founded by Arthur
Waskow.

Rainbow Sign: c/o Menorah/Public Resource Center, 7041 McCallum
Street, Philadelphia, PA 19119.

A creative and exciting Jewish project to prevent nuclear holocaust.

Jewish Peace Center: c/o Stephen Wise Free Synagogue, 30 West 68th
Street, New York, NY 10024.

A coalition of synagogues and Jewish secular organizations dedicated to nuclear disarmament, founded by Rabbi Balfour Brickner
in 1982 and headquartered at his temple. The center convenes
Jewish/interreligious peace conferences, publishes and dissemi-
nates peace sermons and prayers, and offers draft counseling.

Jewish Coalition for a Peaceful World: Suite 402, 702 Franklin Street,
Boston, MA 02110.

A new organization, fostered by the American Jewish Congress,
New England Region. The coalition is united behind the following
Statement of Principle, adapted from the Resolution on a Halt to
the Nuclear Arms Race, passed by the General Assembly of the
Council of Jewish Federations in 1982:

There is a growing concern within our community about the
continuing nuclear arms race. The prospect of nuclear war is
becoming more real and threatening as time goes on.
  We declare that there is a special Jewish viewpoint on this
issue. For us, discussion of a nuclear holocaust is more than a

metaphor. Our history demonstrates that man is capable of perpetrating unspeakable acts on other men and further, that silence in the face of inhumanity is equivalent to complicity.

We call upon all nuclear powers, but especially the United States and the USSR, to pursue a program that will produce a total and multilateral halt to the nuclear arms race.

Within our community, we seek to increase awareness and promote programs addressing the threat of nuclear war.

The Jewish Coalition for a Peaceful World will serve as a network of organizations and individuals striving to achieve these goals.

Jewish Educators for Social Responsibility: 23 Garden Street, Cambridge, MA 02138.

JESR now has available a draft copy of *Nuclear Education and the Jewish Festivals,* which constitutes vol. 1 of its more extensive project. "Jewish Education and the Nuclear Threat." Every volume in this project will offer themes, ideas, and implementation which connect social responsibility to a specific aspect of Jewish education. The goal of the project is to integrate the theme of social responsibility with the already existing educational curricula in Jewish schools.

Start Your Own Group

If your high school or college does not have a Jewish peace group or a CO group, start your own. If it does, become an active participant in it. To start a Jewish peace group ask your Hillel or local rabbi to serve as its resource person. You will also want to affiliate your group with Hillel, to connect with the Jewish community on campus and recruit participants from its ranks. (You should also affiliate with the Jewish Peace Fellowship.) Recruit sympathetic faculty members. Ask them to announce your group in their classes. Give the group's establishment good publicity and talk it up around your school.

If there are too few Jews in your school or college, make it a broad, nonsectarian group, something which you might want to do anyway. Approach your campus chaplain for help, in the absence of a rabbi.

Within your peace group, discuss ideological, spiritual,

moral, ethical, and practical issues relating to conscientious objection. Include some of the difficult questions we are raising in this book like those about the Holocaust and the State of Israel. Read and criticize one another's CO essays. Support each other in your beliefs. Sponsor campus-wide programs on nonviolence and conscientious objection.

While at college, you should try to take any courses available on the history and philosophy of nonviolence. Such courses might be offered by any number of departments, such as sociology, politics or government, history, religion, philosophy, or American studies. If no course exists, join with members of your CO group in petitioning for its establishment. Meanwhile, organize such a course on an informal basis. Do it through your Hillel Foundation or the chaplaincy on your campus. Such courses, both formal and informal, will contribute a great deal to your campus community. This is especially true at schools that host ROTC or "military science" programs and thus need to provide a perspective on nonviolence as well.

On campus, ascertain whether the chaplaincy and/or the faculty senate has taken a strong moral position against university or college compliance with the Solomon Amendment. This piece of congressional legislation requires college administrations to report proof of each student's Selective Service registration as a necessary condition for the student's receiving federal financial aid. If you find that strong moral opposition to such compliance has not been sufficiently raised within your academic community, lobby and organize for it. Encourage the student government, campus newspapers, and other student groups to come out against compliance. Urge faculty members and the chaplains to oppose compliance.

I offer the following statement, issued at Brandeis University by the chaplaincy, as one model for such a position.

> In the unanimous view of the Chaplaincy Department, the Solomon Amendment, which requires colleges and universities to secure and report proof of a student's Selective Service registration as a necessary condition of his receiving federal financial aid, should be opposed and resisted by Brandeis University. Our

counsel grows out of the religious and moral convictions which we share and reflect on campus. In separate statements, our respective traditions and religious institutions have repeatedly expressed opposition to the method of registration propounded by the Solomon Amendment and to draft registration itself. As members of a united campus chaplaincy, we identify especially with the joint religious statement, "Enlighten Our Conscience," the text of which follows (in part):*

We call upon all Americans, especially upon those in positions of power, to reflect upon whether true national security can be accomplished through preparation for war or rather through God's command to act justly. We urge all American young people to consider seriously the moral implications of registration for the military draft. We pledge our pastoral support to those who choose nonregistration for reasons of conscience. We urge young Americans to consider conscientious objector status should the draft be reinstituted. Those who choose to serve in the military should be mindful of the moral implications of the use of indiscriminate weaponry which our country stands ready to use against every woman, man and child in an adversary nation.

During these dark times may the God of truth enlighten our consciences to do the works that make for peace.

The Solomon Amendment converts the university into a law enforcement agency, since its intent is to punish students who, for whatever reasons, have not complied with the draft registration law or are unwilling to certify that they have done so. If universities accept this role, they may well be subject to endless cooptation and manipulation by the federal government in the future. They lose whatever claims to independence they presently have. (Although different in some important respects, this law is nonetheless reminiscent of the Vietnam War regulation which required universities to report the class standing of male students as a means of determining who could be drafted for

---

*"Enlighten Our Conscience," a religious statement on registration for the draft, issued on July 20, 1980 by a coalition of Jewish, Catholic, and Protestant religious and peace groups.

military service. That regulation was rightly opposed by many academicians and universities. As a result, it was rescinded.)

The Solomon Amendment should be opposed first of all, therefore, because it makes of educational institutions an arm of the federal government in general and of the Selective Service System and the Department of Justice in particular. This is antithetical to the goals of higher learning, the proper educational functions of the university. The striving for academic excellence and the pursuit of "truth into its innermost parts" are goals which are incompatible with the requirements with which the Solomon Amendment saddles the university.

Moreover, it is self-evident that the Solomon Amendment is flagrantly discriminatory. For one, it spares women and victimizes only male students, inasmuch as draft registration is required solely of men. Even more serious and repugnant are the invidious class distinctions which the Amendment perpetrates. The law is obviously of no relevance or concern to the affluent, who can pay their way thanks to their families' largesse. It penalizes only the less advantaged (non-registrants) who depend upon (federal) financial aid for the completion of their educations. Further scrutiny will reveal whether the Amendment is racist too. Whether or not these discriminatory dimensions will ultimately suffice to render the Amendment unconstitutional, it is, in our view, both morally inappropriate and educationally inconsistent for the university to involve itself in complicity with any such forms of discrimination.

Finally, it is well known that the reasons many students have not registered for the draft are conscientious ones, reflecting a serious exercise of intellectual and moral responsibility. University officials may or may not agree with the conclusions that these students have reached, though, in our view, the translation of humanistic values and educational truths into this-worldly action merits the academy's praise, at least in principle. Surely, however, the university should not allow itself to be put in the position of helping to impose penalties on those who, after serious moral reflection, have made a difficult and risky moral choice. If punitive measures for civil disobedience are to be imposed, let them proceed properly, through the judicial system, with proper guarantees of due process, etc.

The response Brandeis is considering, namely to provide alternative funds to students who fail to qualify for federal funds under this law, is a well-intentioned but inadequate response in our eyes. It is insufficient because it is a meliorative action which does not confront in a principled way an unprincipled and improper law. It is also insufficient because it is likely that the terms under which students will receive the alternative funds will be significantly less favorable than the terms of the federal aid (e.g., higher interest, necessity to begin repayments while still in college). It cannot be expected that most schools will follow the commendable lead of Amherst College in providing alternative financial assistance on precisely the same terms for students who lose their federal funding, inasmuch as this would obviously cost colleges more than they could bear at a time of severe financial stringency.

It is not clear what the consequences of non-cooperation with the Amendment would be. Threats of withdrawal of federal funds of all kinds have been mentioned. Perhaps they would be implemented. It is more likely that they would not, if a number of major colleges and universities make clear their principled opposition to the law. Our hope is that Brandeis will join hands with Swarthmore, Earlham, Haverford, Harvard, the University of Minnesota and other institutions that are opposing the Solomon Amendment.

The constitutionality of the Solomon Amendment is presently being contested in the courts. A federal district judge in Minnesota has issued a preliminary injunction against implementation of the law on the grounds that there is *prima facie* evidence that the law violates the constitutional provision against self-incrimination. It is desirable that further legal action contesting the law be pursued in other regions. We propose that Brandeis initiate court action, either alone or in concert with other colleges and universities in this area. It is desirable as well that this university and others undertake lobbying efforts for the repeal of the law.

In short, we believe that it would be unconscionable for the university to cooperate in any way with the implementation of the Solomon Amendment.

If you succeed with your peace group, branch out. Encourage the formation of peace groups in other schools or colleges near you. Your knowledge is valuable and should be shared with others who do not know anything about nonviolence, conscientious objection, or draft laws. Speak to high-school-age youth groups at nearby synagogues, churches, YMCAs, or boys' clubs. Try to talk to inner-city groups of high school youths at their schools, churches, or housing projects. Usually, the youths of the inner city are economically disadvantaged and are the least familiar with conscientious objection. Your exposing them to the option of conscientious objection may compensate somewhat for the discrimination which our economic system imposes on them. You may succeed in interesting others in nonviolence too, and, at the very least, you will be raising important questions in your school and its surrounding areas.

Return to your high school for a visit, if you are in college. Find out if justice is being done to COs and all those who have to confront registration. (Make sure this is happening in the schools around your college as well.) Find out, for example, if the communities where these schools are located require that all information on every aspect of draft registration is provided to all high school students. This should include, of course, information on conscientious objection and alternative views on federal policies. Very few communities have such requirements, and it is appropriate for COs, civil libertarians, peace activists, and interested citizens to mobilize and lobby for them.

Approach local school committees to press for the passage of resolutions like the following, which was passed by the Brookline, Massachusetts, school committee (and modeled on resolutions passed in San Francisco and Berkeley).

> . . . It is evident that allowing military recruitment and registration without presentation of alternative views is not in the best interest of Brookline students. . . . appropriate informational materials, listings of resources, speakers and community counseling groups [must] also be available to students, teachers, counselors and parents at Brookline High School.

All school committees should be encouraged to take similar action.

Work with your CO group and others to watch over federal and state legislative trends as they relate to the draft. There are several ominous draft-related federal and state bills pending in various legislatures. Among these are one that would require high schools to give lists of students' names to the Selective Service. This would make it easier for that agency to recruit students and to locate those who have not registered. At present, the schools may decide on their own whether or not to supply such lists. Your group should be aware of the choices the schools in your area have made. Organize against this practice if it is occurring. And join in opposition to any legislation that would make it mandatory for the schools to do so.

Find out whether the high schools in your area or back home sponsor "armed services days" through their career offices. These give representatives of all branches of the military a chance to hand out literature to high school students. Try to stop this practice. If you can't, at least have representatives and materials from groups like Parents Against the Draft or American Friends Service Committee presented to the students as well.

Find out if the guidance counselors or other faculty people at the various high schools you are monitoring encourage students to take the Armed Services Vocational Aptitude Battery during school hours or after. This is said to be a worthwhile aptitude test to be taken before college. But what students are frequently unaware of is that in taking this test they are supplying the military with personal data that is helpful for its recruitment purposes.

In addition to CO groups on campus, join nuclear arms control groups as well, and be active in them. If such groups do not exist on your campus, organize and start them. Examples of such groups are United Campuses to Prevent Nuclear War (UCAM), on a national and local basis, and Students for Nuclear Arms Control (SNAC) on a local basis.

Be active for your own sake and for the benefit of future

generations. All of this peace group and conscientious objector activity will be worthwhile to you and to the general cause of nonviolence. Your work in this area will underline your commitment to the cause of peace and will contribute to the public's understanding of your cause. Your free time during your school years could not be better spent.

The Induction Process

The Random Sequence Number

As I have already said, once you have registered with Selective Service nothing will happen until a draft is reinstated. At that time you will be assigned a Random Sequence Number (RSN), or lottery number. You will receive this number in the year you turn nineteen. All young men born in the same year as you will receive an RSN by lottery according to their birth dates. The numbers range from 1 to 365 (or 366 during a leap year). There is no way to predict what Random Sequence Number you will get. Each number is assigned to a date in the year by a random process. Your birthday may be October 27, but your number could be 1. Or your birthday may be January 1, but your number could be 349. Your Random Sequence Number will stay with you throughout the period during which you are eligible for induction. It will determine the order in which you are called.

Induction

During the year in which you turn twenty, should the draft be reinstated, you will enter the "age 20 selection group" for induction. All men age twenty in that year will be eligible for induction. The call-up works as follows: The Pentagon decides how large an armed force it needs for that year and requests a certain number of men from Selective Service. Since each Random Sequence Number represents several thousand twenty-year-olds, once the number of draftees needed for that year has been determined, Selective Service establishes an

57

"induction cutoff" number and expects to draft everyone through that number. If the cutoff number is 175, then every twenty-year-old with a lottery number from 1 to 175 can be expected to receive his induction notice during that year.

How would this affect you? If your lottery number were below 175, you would receive induction orders and a 1-A (available for military duty) classification. If your number were above 175, and you were not inducted during your selection year, you would drop into the "age 21 selection group" and would only be called after all those in the next year's age-twenty group had been called. Since this isn't likely to happen, you would only have had to worry about induction for one year.

Submit Claim for CO Classification

What if you are inducted? As mentioned above, your induction notice will tell you that you have been classified 1-A: available for military duty. You will have ten days from the date of its mailing to report for induction or request a deferment or exemption. This is the time for you to submit an application requesting conscientious objector status (or any other exemption or deferment as well). Your application must be received by the draft board before your induction date. This is your first real chance to notify Selective Service legally of your position as a conscientious objector.

When you have submitted your initial claim as a conscientious objector, your induction date will be postponed while your case is being considered. You will receive the forms and requirements for your final claim and a date for a personal appearance before your draft board. Upon receiving your forms, rewrite your essay according to the current questions asked, unless you have been able to obtain the written form before this time. If your essay is already written, refine it. Then choose the best of your support letters and bring everything to your draft counselor. Have your counselor look over your materials and help you prepare for your personal appearance.

The Personal Appearance

Appearing before your draft board gives you the chance to present your claim and show your sincerity. You may take up to three witnesses with you for your hearing. (In fact, you should have a witness with you on every visit to your draft board.) You may also take an "adviser" or draft counselor with you. Good choices for this would be your Hillel or hometown rabbi, a lawyer friend, a teacher, or an administrator. Your adviser is not there to represent you—only you can present your own case—but to confer with and advise you on any difficult questions that may be asked.

Be relaxed and optimistic. Dress neatly in whatever you feel comfortable wearing. Don't be sloppy. Assume that as an honest and sincere person who truly believes in nonviolence, you will receive CO status. At the same time, don't be too casual or complacent. You are likely to be asked some difficult questions and should be ready to think carefully and answer thoughtfully. Don't prepare set answers for yourself. A sincere but not quite worked-out statement is better than a programmed, too pat answer. Do the best you can. The important thing to make clear is that you object to war on moral and religious grounds.

As a Jew you should anticipate being asked some difficult questions that relate to Jewish history, teachings, and traditions. These questions are difficult because on the surface they seem to suggest that Judaism is inconsistent with conscientious objection. In the next chapter, I have included some of the most common ones that are asked. They are serious questions for serious people. Some of them have weighed heavily on the minds of Jews, even dissuading them unnecessarily from conscientious objection.

After grappling with these questions, you will have deepened your own Jewish learning as well as your understanding of yourself and how you came to believe as you do.

One further thought: While pondering these Jewish questions, remember that your draft board will not be prepared to engage in long, in-depth discussions with you about them. Don't try to memorize the answers to them. My explanations are only meant to help educate you about them. Also, no one expects you to be a talmudic scholar, unless you are one. Try to understand the essence of Jewish thought and tradition behind each question and answer it in your own words. Your beliefs and feelings will be the most important and the most convincing answers the board can hear.

Some Jewish Questions and Discussions

Question: Doesn't Judaism insist that people should defend themselves, even with violence, in the face of an assault, and repel by force an attack against anyone else? Wouldn't you fight against an attacker to save your own life and the lives of those dear to you?

Discussion: Judaism does provide for self-defense, but this has nothing to do with war and conscientious objection. In order to be a CO, one must be opposed to war, i.e., violence on a collective, national level, not necessarily to violence on the individualized level in a situation of self-defense. In other words, in order to qualify as a CO, it is *not* necessary or required to be an absolute pacifist, i.e., one who would not defend oneself by the force of the fist as an individual.

According to Judaism, attacks are to be repulsed with an absolutely minimal level of violence. One is to prevent an assault by restraining or, if necessary injuring rather than killing the assailant. A person who exerts more violence than is necessary in stopping an attacker is culpable according to Jewish law. Rabbinic sources would have us "be of the persecuted rather than of the persecutors," and Jewish prayer admonishes us to accept taunts and curses silently rather than strike back in kind. These and other comparable admonitions have been underscored in many essays on Judaism, most notably in Reuven Kimelman's perceptive article, "Nonviolence in the Talmud," published in the JPF volume, *Roots of Jewish Nonviolence.*

Question: Wasn't Abraham willing to sacrifice and slaughter his son Isaac, and isn't he praised for his obedience and willingness to do so?

Discussion: Abraham was willing, but the Torah describes this as a "test" of Abraham. In characteristic abhorrence of child sacrifice, which was rampant throughout the ancient east, God would not have permitted this of Abraham. (There are even some Jewish interpreters who think that the story really represents Abraham's testing of God.) A particularly interesting Jewish teaching points out that while it is God who commands Abraham to sacrifice Isaac, according to the biblical account, it is "only" an angel who interferes and commands Abraham to refrain from doing so. This teaching concludes that one may kill only at the direct command of God, but one is to refrain from killing even at the command of a "mere" angel. In fact, according to Judaism, the shedding of blood is of such ultimate seriousness and consequence that the rabbis of the Talmud taught that one who kills a single person is accountable for slaying a multitude, and conversely, one who saves a single individual is responsible for saving the whole world.

Question: Consider all the wars and fighting heroes of the Old Testament. How can you, as a Jew, be a conscientious objector?

Discussion: The Hebrew Bible does indeed contain a history of wars, but ancient Judaism only countenanced wars of two main varieties: *milchemet reshut,* an optional or permissible war, and *milchemet mitzvah* or *milchemet chovah,* an obligatory or mandatory war. Foremost among the first category were wars of expansion and territorial aggrandizement, e.g., most of the wars waged by the biblical kings. Inasmuch as such wars require the authorization of the Sanhedrin (Great Court), long extinct, they may not be fought in our day and are, therefore, of academic interest alone. As for the second category, mandatory or obligatory war, this was of three types, only the third of which is of practical relevance to us today. The first type of mandatory war was the battle Israel was commanded to mount against the nation of Amalek, which had attacked the stragglers of our people from the rear during our escape from slavery in ancient Egypt. We were commanded in the Bible to annihilate that nation completely. As Amalek has been extinct for many centuries, this type of war is solely of academic interest (although, exercising their homiletical license, rabbis have been known to claim all too facilely that Amalek is alive and well, in different personifications, from generation to generation). The second type of mandatory war is similarly of academic interest exclusively, inasmuch as this war of total obliteration was to be waged against the seven Canaanite nations, all of them also long extinct. In terms of our real world, then, that leaves for practical consideration only the third kind of mandatory war, namely, the war of collective self-defense, a war in defense of the very existence and survival of the Jewish people. In real terms you need to consider how likely and possible it is for such a war to occur in *today's* world—not centuries ago, not even decades ago.

Furthermore, Judaism developed from the Bible and is not limited to it. The Bible itself yearned for and envisioned peace and demanded that the Jew pursue it. This is a central *mitzvah*, or commandment, in the Bible. In fact, of traditional Judaism's 613 commandments, only justice and peace are not merely to be fulfilled in one's dwelling place but to be actively pursued everywhere. Prophets and psalmists in the Bible railed against the entering of military alliances and involvements and the reliance on might and weaponry. They urge trust in God. Jewish tradition over the centuries cultivated an aversion to war, killing, and bloodshed, so much so that the communal Confessional for the Day of Atonement couples violence ("strength of hand") with the profanation of God's name. The Bible and later Jewish sources put restraining limits on war even when it could be fought. These included bans on defoliation, on sneak attacks, and on surrounding a besieged city on all sides. Such restraints are obviously naive and laughable in terms of modern warfare.

Biblical exemptions from the military are also interesting to note. The Book of Deuteronomy exempts the newlywed, the owners of new, unconsecrated homes and vineyards, and, finally, the man who is "afraid and tender-hearted." One talmudic interpretation takes this latter category to imply two separate exemptions—"afraid" meaning those who are weak and fearful, and "tender-hearted" meaning those who are physically robust but so gentle and compassionate as to be unsuitable for service as warriors. Such persons, classical Judaism's equivalent to the modern CO, are exempt from serving in the military.

According to chapter 31 of the biblical Book of Numbers, especially verses 19–20 and 24, Israelite soldiers were considered to be ritually unclean and impure after battle. In fact they were considered to have incurred the very highest degree of impurity, comparable to one who had touched a corpse. In the same biblical chapter, the Torah describes the purification process that soldiers underwent after battle. All who had participated in the act of killing remained outside the Israelite camp for seven days, during which they engaged in the process of ritual purification. This process included the washing of the garment that they had worn during the war and the ritual cleansing of their bodies. What this indicates is that killing in war was considered to be the most severe kind of defilement of the human body.

Finally, the Jewish attitude toward relating to one's enemy is clearly inconsistent with military means. It is especially incompatible with wartime values. Illustrative of Judaism's orientation is the biblical teaching, "Rejoice not when your enemy falls, and let not your heart exult when he stumbles; lest the Lord see it and be displeased, and He turn away His wrath from him," (Proverbs 24: 17-18). In tractate *Baba Metzia* (32b), the Babylonian Talmud teaches that "if two claim your help, and one is an enemy, help him first." Centuries later, an eighteenth-century Hasidic teaching had it that Rabbi Michal gave this command to his sons: "Pray for your enemies that all may be well with them. And rest assured that, far from opposing God's will, these prayers of yours more than any others will be in God's service."

In this vein, the teachings of Martin Buber, one of the preeminent Jewish religious thinkers of the twentieth century, come to mind. In his major work, *I And Thou*, Buber taught that we must address and relate to one another not as objects but as subjects, as "Thou"s rather than as "It"s. This Jewish teaching precludes thinking of other human beings as enemies deserving of hatred and destruction. The Buberian view of interpersonal relations is consistent with classical Judaism, which, among other things, likened even such offenses as the public embarrassment and humiliation of another person and the spreading of malicious gossip to murder. (Ibn Ezra, the great medieval rationalist, suggested that the imperative "Thou shalt not murder," found in the Decalogue, or Ten Commandments, includes not only murder by physical weapons but murder through the use of speech as well.) Such teachings find their earlier culmination in the various synopses of the Torah offered by several of the talmudic sages. Rabbi Akiba, for example, suggested that the imperative "Love thy fellow as thyself" (Leviticus 19:18) represents the heart of the Torah. Alternatively, Hillel taught that the essence of Torah may be summarized in the mandate "What is hateful to you do not do to your fellow." "All the rest," said Hillel, "is commentary. Go and study it."

Question: In order for the Hebrews to become free from slavery in ancient Egypt, wasn't violence necessary in the form of killing Egypt's firstborn and drowning the pursuing Egyptian army?

Discussion: Yes, but those were divinely imposed measures in which the Israelites themselves did not physically participate, as has been pointed out emphatically in Rabbi Aaron Samuel Tamaret's beautiful essay "Passover and Nonviolence," translated by Rabbi Everett Gendler, and published in the JPF paperback, *Roots of Jewish Nonviolence*. Furthermore, at the Passover *seder*, when the ten plagues of Egypt are recited, we Jews observe the ritual of pouring wine from our goblets at the recitation of each plague. This is done to reduce our rejoicing and to symbolize our commiseration with the suffering Egyptians, even though they were our enemy and deserved punishment for having tyrannized us. For a similar reason, a set of celebratory psalms called Hallel (meaning "praise" of God) is abbreviated on the Passover holyday.

In this way and others as well, the Bible's slavery account and its interpretation convey the repugnance of violence in Judaism's eyes. For example, the biblical Book of Exodus portrays a scene in which Moses, who is out walking in a field, spies in the distance two Hebrew slaves fighting. Moses scolds the evildoer, "Why do you strike your fellow?" The rabbis of old wondered how Moses could possibly have known who was the evildoing perpetrator and who was the innocent victim. After all, he had seen everything only from a distance. Their response was that the one who had his hand raised in readiness to hit the other at the time Moses drew near was the one who was addressed as the evildoer. This response was intended to teach us that even the very pose of preparing to strike a blow, the posture of raising the clenched fist, is sufficient to stigmatize one as an evildoer, whether or not the blow is actually delivered.

Question: How about King David? Wasn't he a great warrior? He fought even as a child (the Goliath incident). Wasn't he also a model king? And isn't the Messiah to come from his seed?

Discussion: True, King David fought many wars and was also a great king. But the Bible sought to understate his militarism and omitted all mention of many of his military exploits. We know about them from other ancient Near Eastern sources, not from the Bible. As for the Bible itself, in its pages King David was denied the one thing he wanted most of all, namely, to build the first Holy Temple in Jerusalem. He was denied that singular distinction because his hands were too filled with blood. The honor went instead to his son Solomon, ancient Israel's third king, whose Hebrew name, Shlomo, contains the word *shalom*, which means "peace, wholeness, completion."

(The Hebrew *shalom* reflects not only the absence of war, as in the Latin *pax*, but the only whole or complete state.)

Jewish postbiblical sources focus on and praise King David not so much for heroism in battle as for his piety, his learning, and his sweet, soothing music, which is also highlighted in the Bible. We Jews remember King David traditionally as "the sweet singer of Israel" and as the author of many psalms in the biblical Book of Psalms.

Question: Thanks to a television spectacular and a best-selling novel, we are now very much aware of the brave Jewish warriors of centuries ago who resisted the Roman Empire and died courageous deaths by suicide on Masada. Don't you identify with those brave heroes?

Discussion: While we all very much respect the Jewish warriors of Masada and mourn their deaths, as we do the deaths of all our martyrs, it seems to many of us that the struggle at Masada that ended so tragically in mass suicide was futile. Had all the Jews of that day been with Eleazar ben Yair and his Zealot followers it would have been the end of the Jewish people.

Providentially, that was not the case. At about the same time that Eleazar ben Yair and his followers went atop Masada, another Jewish leader of that day, Rabban (Rabbi) Yochanan ben Zakkai, a pious and learned scholar, decided to pursue a totally different course of action in the grave struggle for Jewish survival. Yochanan ben Zakkai's alternative was to take the option of active spiritual resistance. He appeared before the Roman commander, Vespasian, acknowledged the impending fall of Jerusalem, and bargained for Israel's future. For his people, the heroic Yochanan ben Zakkai requested and received permission for one thing—namely, "Yavneh and her scholars," that is, the authorization to found a yeshiva, an academy of Jewish learning and scholarship in the town of Yavneh (Jamnia). Other academies of learning were established by other sages following Yochanan ben Zakkai's lead. It was the model of Yavneh, not of Masada, that became the guarantor of the spiritual survival of the Jewish people and the continuity of Judaism. In the Yavneh model, emphasis on Jewish learning and spirituality replaced the stress on Jewish political nationalism and military resistance that was central in the Masada model. Without deprecating the heroism of Masada's brave warriors, it is fair to say that it is the contemporaneous Yavneh model of spiritual resistance and the heroism of Yochanan ben Zakkai and the sages that we can thank for the perpetuation of Judaism and the people Israel during the Roman period.

Question: How about the Maccabees, the great warriors who defeated the Syro-Greek Empire in an armed revolt? Doesn't Judaism have a holyday called Hanukkah to honor them and their military victory?

Discussion: Yes, but the celebration of Hanukkah does not really treat the Maccabees' miraculous triumph over the Syro-Greek armies as its sole, central theme. It is rather a spiritual holyday, in keeping with Judaism's highest ideals, that underscores yet another miracle. Hanukkah celebrates the cleansing and rededication of the Holy Temple after it had been contaminated and defiled by the Syro-Greeks. The word *hanukkah* means "dedication" and refers to the miracle of the tiny amount of undefiled oil that burned in the Temple's rededication not for one day, as was expected, but for eight days. (The Babylonian Talmud's discussion may be found in *Shabbat* 21–24). That is the meaning, too, of the other name for Hanukkah, namely, the Festival of Lights. Hanukkah is also celebrated to commemorate the refusal of the Jews to bend the knee to false gods like the Syro-Greek king and their reaffirmation of their loyalty to the one true God.

The theme of the Festival of Lights is capped by the rabbinic teaching (*Pesikta Rabbati,* chap. 2) that begins with the question, "Why do we light candles on Hanukkah?" The response is that after the Maccabean victory, the Hasmoneans (Judah Maccabee and his family) "entered the Temple and found eight iron spears. They pounded them [into the ground] and kindled lights in them." This rabbinic story about the first Hanukkah menorah reflects the Jewish spiritual ideal of transforming war into peace, swords into plowshares, spears into God-serving instruments. As though to emphasize this point even further, the Haftarah (prophetic reading appended to the weekly Torah portion) chanted on the very Sabbath of Hanukkah highlights the biblical prophet Zechariah's pertinent reminder, "Not by might and not by power, but by My spirit, saith the Lord of Hosts."

Question: What about capital punishment? Doesn't the Bible demand the use of the death penalty?

Discussion: The question is altogether extraneous and has nothing whatever to do with war and conscientious objection. Nonetheless, let us address it.

In theory, the Hebrew Bible certainly does allow for capital punishment, prescribing it, for example, for the crime of murder. As has been clear throughout the discussion in this chapter, however, in order to understand Judaism properly, one must look beyond the Bible. Judaism is a cumulative tradition that evolved and developed over many centuries. It started with the germinating seed we call the Bible but went beyond it. To understand Judaism properly one must learn the Bible and add to it the teachings of the subsequent centuries of the tradition.

Like all concepts, the subject of capital punishment must be considered with this in mind. Thus, while the Hebrew Bible prescribes capital punishment, it is of greater importance to note that the subsequent teachings virtually interpreted the death penalty out of existence. Actually convicting a murderer, for example, was made into an extremely complex matter. The talmudic rabbis insisted that the court prove beyond a doubt premeditation on the part of the murderer. All forms of circumstantial evidence were inadmissable. A minimum of two witnesses was required of the prosecution. One of the most prominent of the rabbis, Simeon ben Shetach, who presided over the Sanhedrin (Great Court) during the reigns of King Alexander Yannai and Queen Salome Alexandra (76–69 B.C.E.), reported the following story: "I witnessed one man pursuing another into a ruin. Running after him, I saw in his hand a sword dripping with the victim's blood, with the victim writhing in the agony of death. I charged him [the perpetrator]: 'You villain!! Who killed this person? [Obviously] it was either you or me! But what can I do [inasmuch as I am the sole witness]!!' [The Torah requires that] according to the utterance of two witnesses shall the one who deserves death be executed!"

As for the two witnesses, in addition to having observed the murder, it was further required that they warn the perpetrator of the consequences of the murder and of the specific type of capital punishment to be meted out for the crime. Under no circumstances could a verdict be pronounced and a sentence executed on the basis of the murderer's confession alone. Moreover, the character of the witnesses was also a factor. They had to be decent and trustworthy men. Questionable moral characters, including usurers and gamblers, were ruled to be unqualified as judges and as witnesses. Finally, witnesses were subject to a difficult cross-examination, and the judge was encouraged to interfere as much as possible. Rabbinic sources have it that "the more a judge tests the testimony, the more praiseworthy is he."

In trying the alleged murderer, neither the local court nor the relatively more centralized court was sufficient. Rather, the Sanhedrin (the Great Court composed of twenty-three judges) was required. And there it took a split decision to sentence the culprit to death. A unanimous decision might mean that prejudice was involved. To convict a murderer, a majority of at least two was required by law. On the other hand, to acquit, a majority of one was quite sufficient.

After considering all this, it should come as no surprise that historically Jewish courts very rarely meted out capital punishment. The Talmud is on record as having declared that "a Sanhedrin that executes one man in seven years was called a killing court." To this definition one noted talmudic sage, Rabbi Eliezer ben Azariah, appended, "Or one man in even seventy years," to which the great rabbinic pair of Rabbis Akiba and

Tarfon added, "Had we sat on the Sanhedrin, no one would ever have been put to death!"

There are some who maintain that the talmudic rabbis' compassionate outlook is a function of the historical reality that Jewish (rabbinic) courts had, in fact, been stripped of the authority to levy the death penalty some forty years before the Holy Temple's destruction at the hands of the Romans. These cynics suggest that inasmuch as the whole issue was nothing more than academic, theoretic, or hypothetical by that time, rabbinic sources could afford to be magnanimous and kindly. I believe that the compassionate outlook of the rabbinic courts reflects the humanitarian and life-affirming values that permeate Jewish teachings. The infinite preciousness and sanctity of human life has been a constant in the history of the Jewish tradition.

Question: Doesn't the Bible's administration of justice allow for violent punishment? "An eye for an eye and a tooth for a tooth" doesn't sound much like a nonviolent tradition!

Discussion: Again, this too has nothing to do with conscientious objection. As to the issue, Judaism never took the phrase "an eye for an eye and a tooth for a tooth" literally. Instead, it was taken to mean "the *value* of an eye for an eye, the *value* of a tooth for a tooth." The Talmud devised a comprehensive system of compensation based on such things as medical costs, pain, unemployment, and other results of injury for determining the value of an eye for an eye and a tooth for a tooth.

Question: Judaism isn't a vegetarian tradition. Doesn't allowing the eating of meat indicate that Jews were never intended to be conscientious objectors?

Discussion: To begin with, one does not have to be a vegetarian in order to be a CO. One does not follow from the other. As for Judaism, it is true that the tradition permits the eating of meat. In so doing, however, Judaism may be making a concession or accommodation to human weakness rather than promoting the eating of meat as the ideal. In fact, though it allowed the eating of meat, Judaism forbade the eating of certain animals, like the pig. This limited the kinds of meat we may eat. Moreover, Judaism prohibited the eating of blood because it is the very being, the essence of life.

Compassion for animal life, known in Hebrew as *tsa'ar ba'alei chayyim*, which is partially at the root of the Jewish aversion to the sport of hunting, is an important value in Judaism. It advises that one should feed one's animal before oneself and prohibits the Jew from inflicting even the slightest pain on any animal, much less kill it for sport. In fact, Jewish law also developed a unique and stringent system of humane animal slaughter laws designed to spare the animal undue pain and suffering.

As an aside, it is interesting to note that while Jewish law requires the recitation of the *Shehecheyanu*, a blessing thanking God for all milestones and momentous occasions, and recited whenever one puts on a brand-new garment for the first time, among other things, it bans that very blessing when the new item is a pair of shoes made of leather. On our holiest of days, Yom Kippur (the Day of Atonement), traditional Jews do not wear anything made of leather, for which an animal's life was obviously taken. Considering all this, it should not come as a surprise that the Society for the Prevention of Cruelty to Animals was founded by a Jew, the Englishman Lewis Gompertz.

Question: What about Hitler and the Nazis? Wouldn't you fight them? Wouldn't you be ashamed of people who allowed themselves to be led meekly like sheep to the slaughter?

Discussion: No one can say what he or she would have done at that time. How could a person know? While Hitler was rebuilding Germany, reforming its social institutions, and speaking out against communism, the Western world admired him. On the other hand, most people today would probably say they would have fought him. (For more on this point, read *So You Would Have Fought Hitler* by Arlo Tatum, available from the Central Committee for Conscientious Objectors.) Hindsight makes all of Hitler's atrocities perfectly clear. As a CO, however, you do not have to decide what you would have done at any time in the past or in the future. You can only know what you must do now. No more can legally or morally be expected of you.

As for people meekly standing by or being led to slaughter, there was much nonviolent resistance to Hitler on the part of the people of Europe and the Jews themselves. Many Europeans hid threatened Jews from the Nazis. The people of Denmark smuggled almost their entire Jewish population out of the country and into Sweden when German occupation was imminent.

As for the Jewish victims—many engaged in armed struggle against the Nazis. Others resisted with equal heroism in spiritual and nonviolent ways. Those who could, escaped. When escape was no longer possible, they maintained their dignity and humanity, continued their Jewish learning and observance, engaged in forms of culture, conducted schools for children, cared for one another, and defied the Nazis in many other nonviolent ways. There is no clearer example of such courageous, nonviolent resistance than that of the Polish-Jewish author and educator of young children, Janusz Korczak, who actually founded an orphanage in the Warsaw ghetto. This hero was offered personal freedom, the opportunity to flee, by the Nazis. Loyal to the children of his orphanage, however, Korczak agreed to accept the Nazi offer on one condition— if his orphans could leave with him. The Nazis, of course, refused. Korczak walked to his death in a concentration camp, hand-in-hand with his little orphans, whom he tried to calm and comfort to the very end. Both within and without the concentration camps they resisted. Nonviolence does not mean passivity. It can be active and resistant while refusing to sink to the animal level of the perpetrator.

As for World War II, if it was fought to save the Jewish and other innocent concentration camp victims from the Holocaust, it was a dismal failure. In fact, more than a few Holocaust survivors themselves contend that it was the war itself that permitted the Holocaust. They conclude that, although Hitler had to be resisted and opposed, were it not for the cover provided by World War II, the Nazis might not have gotten away with the perpetration of the Holocaust. They believe that the war effort achieved the silencing of German opposition from within and sabotaged potential intercession on behalf of the civilian victims, Jews and others, from without. Raul Hilberg is not alone among historians and other analysts in pointing to the utilization of war machinery by the Nazis in perpetrating the Holocaust.

Speaking of World War II, let me add parenthetically that you will, no doubt, find considerable interest in Murray's Polner's original oral history of Jewish conscientious objectors during World War II. This oral history project is on file at four different centers, namely, the American Jewish Historical Society (on the campus at Brandeis University, Waltham, MA, 02254); the American Jewish Archives (at Hebrew Union College—Jewish Institute of Religion in Cincinnati, Ohio, 45220); the Swarthmore Peace Collection (Swarthmore, Pa., 19081); and the William E. Weiner Oral History Collection (American Jewish Committee, New York, N.Y., 10022). The American Jewish Historical Society also houses the fine collection of conscientious objection applications and essays gathered by the Jewish Peace Fellowship.

Question: What about Israel? Don't you admire the military heroism of the Israelis? As a Jew, wouldn't you fight in defense of Israel?

Discussion: Make it clear to your draft board that you are both a proud Jew and a proud American. But as a loyal citizen of the United States, it is impossible for you to put yourself in the position of fighting or not fighting in another country's war. As an American and a CO here, it is not a question that you should be expected to answer. Certainly you are a committed, supportive partisan of Israel. For both Jews and Americans, Israel's survival is very important.

One can easily support the idea of a Jewish homeland, however, while believing that various Israeli governments have acted out of character with Jewish tradition. Many people believe the key to Israel's survival and security lies not in military strength and superiority alone, but in establishing peace and normalcy with the neighboring Arab states and the Palestinian people. For a CO this seems to be a fitting goal and a most appropriate emphasis. In Israel itself there is a peace movement that includes the large group known as Peace Now, as well as a branch of War Resisters Internationale. Israel is also the setting of still other small but vital peace groups. Among these are the Israel Interfaith Committee; Yesh G'vul (meaning both "there is a limit," i.e., to Israel's war policy and Lebanese presence, and "there is a boundary," i.e., demarcating Lebanese sovereignty); Oz VeShalom (meaning "strength and peace"), the Israeli Orthodox Zionists for peace; Netivot Shalom (meaning "paths to peace"), also an Orthodox peace movement; the Committee Against the War in Lebanon; the Committee Against Settlement in Hebron; Mizrach HaShalom (meaning "East [or, more precisely, Afro-Asian Jews] for peace"); Soldiers Against Silence; Parents Against Silence; Women Against the Invasion (now known as Women Against the Occupation); and the very eminent research and activist institute based in Tel Aviv, the International Center for Peace in the Middle East, founded by Simha Flapan and presided over by Arie (Lova) Eliav. Of these groups, Yesh G'vul can be described as an enterprise in selective conscientious objection. Its members consist of approximately two thousand reserve soldiers who have put in writing their commitment to refuse to serve military duty in Lebanon, on the basis of their Jewish and human moral codes. Israel's Ministry of Defense has rejected the petition of these soldiers, summoning many of them to serve in Lebanon, in response to which close to one hundred of the soldiers have refused service. Some have been court-martialed and interned in military prisons. Others find alternative ways of avoiding service in Lebanon.

In addition to these groups, there is also a multiplicity of other Israeli organizations struggling for Arab-Jewish reconciliation and cooperation. Among these are Shutafut, meaning "partnership"; Interns for Peace (a Peace Corps–like program involving teams of Arabs and Jews, largely in their mid and late twenties, working and living in several Arab towns); Neve

Shalom (an Arab-Jewish cooperative settlement, which oper-
ates a school for peace); Givat Haviva, in Hadera; Heart-to-
Heart Camp, founded by the World Union for Progressive
Judaism (the Reform movement outside the US), which seeks
to inculcate trust and openness between Arab and Jewish
youngsters in a camp setting; the Van Leer Institute's experimental curriculm, slated to be implemented in fifty Jewish
schools throughout Israel, for the purpose of sensitizing Israeli
youngsters to Arab history and culture; and the Institute for
Education for Co-Existence between Jews and Arabs, co-spon-
sored by the Israeli government. Many of these enterprises
which toil in the pressing vineyard of Arab-Jewish rapprochement are now united in a new network, Reshet, meaning
"net."

From a Jewish peace perspective, it is altogether laudable
that so many peace and reconciliation initiatives transpire in
Israel. One cannot but hope that the government, too, will
become increasingly well disposed toward peace initiatives.
Similarly, one cannot but hope that such peace and reconciliation initiatives, thus far conspicuously missing in Arab countries and among the Palestinian people, will proliferate in those
quarters, too. That would, indeed, be a most salutary development.

There are also conscientious objectors, draft resisters, and
soldiers who refuse to serve elsewhere in occupied territory.
Israeli Army Colonel Eli Geva, a genuine hero in my eyes,
refused to order the soldiers under his command into battle in
Beirut during the Lebanese invasion of 1982. Israel is not a
monolithic country and is divided on the peace issue as well as
many others.

While it is true that in response to Israel's conflicts many
Jews tend to glorify the warrior, Judaism defines genuine
heroism and bravery in terms other than the physical and the
military. In *Pirke Avoth (Ethics of the Fathers)*, the question is
raised, "Who is a hero?" or "Who is strong?" The reply is,
"One who conquers [overcomes, controls] one's passions [ap-
petites, inclinations to do evil]." In another early rabbinic tract,

Avoth d'Rabbi Natan, that question is amplified anew: "Who is the hero among heroes?" or "Who is the strongest among the strong?" This time the response is, "One who makes of one's enemy one's friend."

In the classical Jewish view, courageous heroism is epitomized not in military exploits on the field of battle but in mastery over the self and especially in the effort to harmonize and reconcile strained and soured interpersonal relations. In *Ethics of the Fathers* (1:12), the great sage Hillel advises us to pattern ourselves on the peace-loving model of the biblical Aaron, Moses' brother. Hillel said, "Be of the disciples of Aaron, loving peace and pursuing peace, loving [all of] God's creatures and bringing them near to the Torah [God's law]." The daily (morning) liturgy of the Jew excerpts a mishnaic passage (*Peah* 1:1) that includes mandatory sharings with the poor and the doing of deeds of loving-kindness among the *mitzvot* (commandments, religious duties) for which there is no prescribed measure. This passage is juxtaposed with another talmudic selection (*Shabbat* 127a) that adds the religious duty of peacemaking as one of several other *mitzvot* the performance of which brings both immediate reward in this world and ever-lasting gratification in the world-to-come. Such are the values of the Jewish tradition. As God is merciful and compassionate, so must we be. As God is long-suffering and slow to anger, so must we be. As God is forgiving and easily pacified, so must we be. And so it goes.

God, of course, is seen as the Cosmic Peacemaker par excellence in Judaism. "Maker of peace in His heavens," God is depicted by the rabbis as having intentionally gone out of the way to foster peace in the world at the time of creation. The Midrash teaches, for example, that God purposefully and evenly alternated the creation of celestial and earthly beings through the first six days of creation so as to prevent jealously and quarreling between them. On the seventh day, God created Adam, the earthling, out of both the heavenly and earthly spheres so as to maintain peace and harmony. It is for us to emulate God, the Cosmic Peacemaker. According to Judaism, the imitation of God, *Imitatio Dei*, is the religious task in life, the highroad to holiness.

In preparing to deal with these and other related Jewish questions, consult the informative Jewish sources referred to in the ensuing pages. Of special value is the JPF publication, *The Roots of Jewish Nonviolence*.

Your draft board may include a knowledgeable Jew. It might even include a rabbi. Anticipate such a possibility and don't let it upset you. If you have invited your rabbi to accompany you, and if the board permits it, s/he will know how to respond gently but firmly and authoritatively to the rabbi on the board.

Remember that respectfulness and gentleness are the order of the day. Stress that Judaism is not a monolithic tradition. Pluralism has always pervaded our history. Allow politely that all Jews, including the one on the board, have the right to their own opinions, but that other approaches to Judaism are also valid. The conscientious objector's nonviolent approach is in the spirit of Judaism's aversion to bloodshed. Remember and emphasize that the Talmud (in tractate *Sanhedrin*) is on record as having legislated that there are three offenses that the Jew is forbidden to trangress, even on pain of death. These are bloodshed, idolatry, and adultery. As though to drive the point home more vividly, the Talmud weaves the tale of one who was commanded by the Roman governor of the day to kill a certain person. The governor threatened that if the Jew refused to fulfill the command he would be put to death. The Jew, torn and upset, asked the advice of the great talmudic authority Rabba, who told him in no uncertain terms that he was to forfeit his own life rather than kill the other person on command. "How do you know," asked Rabba, rhetorically, "that your blood is redder than his?" (Maimonides later ruled that if, under such extreme duress, one obeyed the command to kill rather than forfeit life, such a one, though culpable, was not to suffer court-imposed punishment.)

Do stress the latitude and diversity of views and approaches within Judaism. After all, Orthodox, Reform, Conservative, and Reconstructionist Jews differ considerably on matters of

Jewish ideology today. The same was true of the Sadducees and Pharisees, the Hasidim and Mitnagdim, and many other Jewish groups in the distant past. Yet all are embraced within the fellowship of the Jewish people. This cannot be overemphasized, particularly when one considers that some religious traditions and churches are indeed monolithic. It must, therefore, be very carefully explained and stressed that this is not so much a matter of picking and choosing inconsistently as of identifying with a stream of teachings within a pluralistic, nonmonolithic tradition that contains wide variances.

Understand that a Jew on the board may well harbor an insecurity and a fear that Jewish COs will reflect poorly on other Jews. S/he may fear that you and other COs call into question the loyalty and patriotism of Jewish citizens. This fear may account for his/her giving you a hard time. Without directly confronting this fear, assure both him/her and the board that you are loyal to America and desire to serve your country outside the military.

This fear of Jews not being viewed as patriotic citizens is not an uncommon insecurity among Diaspora Jews. Don't be surprised if the Jew on the board is very outspoken about his/her feelings. S/he may ask you quite bluntly, "Don't you believe in loyalty to your country, son? Shouldn't you fulfill your responsibility and serve your country without trying to be a privileged character? If the law of your country provides for military service, shouldn't you obey the law? Doesn't Judaism say that we must obey the law of the society in which we live? Especially as a Jew, don't you appreciate this country and the freedom it affords?" In response you should remain calm and courteous. Assure the board that you are a loyal citizen, that you do appreciate your country and the freedom it affords you, that you are obeying the law by requesting CO status, and that you stand fully prepared to serve your country outside the military.

As for obeying the law of the land in which you live, America defines itself in the Pledge of Allegiance as "one nation under God." This means that God's will is supreme. The Jewish view is in harmony with that. The Talmud asserts that concerning civil matters "the law of the land is law," and Judaism expects us to be loyal, obedient citizens of society. But while obeying civil law, one must never violate God's law, especially with respect to bloodshed, idolatry, and adultery. If the law of the land clashes with the law of God, the Jew must obey God. To obey the law of the land when it conflicts with God's law is to engage in idolatrous behavior. Conclude by summarizing that you are not asking for a special privilege, that you are only seeking to claim your rightful, legal exemption. You are a proud and loyal American who desires to serve his country and humankind.

If you are confronted with other difficult questions, just relax. Answer calmly and rationally. Think over each question before answering respectfully and in religious, moral, or ethical terms. It should be of no small comfort to you that your draft board is not likely to be a group of biblical or Judaica scholars or sophisticated theologians. If someone mentions a point of Jewish history or belief that you are unaware of, do not be afraid to say so. If the values presented seem opposed to yours, do not feel you have to explain the contradiction. Just reiterate that Judaism has been evolving over centuries and that throughout its history it has been a pluralistic religion with room for many points of view.

Throughout your interview try to remain calm. Listen carefully to each question, consult with your adviser if you need to, and answer as clearly as you can. Respond to these Jewish questions as you would respond to any of the draft board's questions—in your own words. It is your beliefs and feelings that need to be expressed at this hearing, not mine. Hopefully the discussions here of difficult Jewish-related questions will help you if your draft board confronts you with any of them.

What If Your Application Is Refused?

Be hopeful and optimistic about the outcome of your claim for classification as a CO. Every bona fide conscientious objector deserves official recognition and the attainment of CO status. If, however, your draft board misses the obvious and commits a blunder, what should you do? Keep calm. Don't be intimidated or demoralized. Keep your spirits up despite your draft board's mistake. (They are only human.) But prepare for non-violent combat.

Find a Good Lawyer or Counselor

In the first place, you have just fifteen days from the time your CO claim is rejected by your local draft board to file your appeal. At this point, you must play by the rules and use the rights you have to pursue your case. Now is the time to find a good draft lawyer or counselor if you haven't already. You can learn a great deal about the appeal process from NISBCO and CCCO literature, but because the Selective Service regulations are subject to change, find an authority who is up to date on draft law.

Draft lawyers are often idealistic men and women who charge modest fees or none at all for their advice. The CCCO can provide the names of good draft attorneys. Or you could ask your hometown or Hillel rabbi or the peace groups mentioned above for recommendations. Inquire at local law schools, the bar association, or synagogues for names. You could also approach Jewish communal relations agencies like the American Jewish Committee, the American Jewish Congress, the Anti-Defamation League, or the local Jewish Community Relations Council for the names of draft lawyers. Write or call the American Civil Liberties Union or the National Lawyers Guild. Ask your Hillel director about lawyers on his/her board or alumni constituency. Whoever you find, make sure that s/he is up to date on Selective Service regulations and conscientious objection and has had experience and shown ability in the field.

If you decide to use a counselor instead of an attorney, consult CCCO or the JPF and AFSC chapters in your area for names. Parents Against the Draft, a relatively new organization, may also be helpful in giving you names.

Know your rights. You have the right to consult your Selective Service file. In fact, with written permission from you, anyone may have access to your file. Whenever you need to know something about your file, don't hesitate to use this right. Your district appeal board may sense how well briefed you are on your rights and the process of appeal. It will realize that you are a worthy opponent and that taking you on may be more trouble than you are worth.

Look to Other Sources If Your Appeal Fails

If your appeal process fails, resourceful efforts on your part may overturn the situation. It is important to go by the rules and use all the rights you have. Follow your lawyer's or counselor's advice, but should things not go well for you in the regular appeal process, start thinking of other ways to win the battle. Make your fight a collaborative affair. Brainstorm with your parents, close relatives and friends, Hillel and hometown rabbis, and professors. They may have some good ideas, or you may want to try any or all of the following:

Initiate a letter-writing campaign by asking your friends and supporters to write elected and appointed officials on your behalf. Have them write your U.S. senators and representatives, your governor, state senators, and representatives, your mayor, selectmen, or aldermen. You want your letter writers to communicate your sincerity and authenticity as a conscientious objector to these officials. You want them to be informed that a grave injustice has been done to you. And you want the officials to intercede on your behalf with your draft board and with the Director of Selective Service in your state by letter, telegram, telephone, or in person. While these political figures may not know you, they will be impressed by the letters from your allies and will do what they can for you. (After all, your letter writers are their constituents.) A few words from the right people can be quite effective. State and local politicians may have contacts on the draft board, and they *do* have power. I am reminded of a CO case some years ago in which a "hawkish" congressman, a senior member of the House Armed Services Committee, interceded on behalf of a young man. Because of his help, the young man's CO appeal was successful.

Once the letters have gone out, have your friends and relatives call the officials or their aides for an update on their efforts. Have them continue to call (without being too aggressive) to keep informed of what is being done for you.

Ask three of your closest advisers or friends to pay a visit, by appointment, to your state's Director of Selective Service. (He is probably a colonel.) If possible, the three should be your Hillel or hometown rabbi, an articulate professor, and a persuasive, forceful friend. Their mission is to convince the Director of your sincerity as a CO and to request a reconsideration of your case. This should be a respectful, civil visit and should come soon after the helpful, interceding efforts of the officials, although precise timing is not necessary.

Start a letter campaign by your friends and allies to your district draft board expressing polite disbelief at the rejection of your appeal. These letters should also ask that your claim be reconsidered to prevent an injustice.

Find a sympathetic, respected investigative reporter in your area and get him or her interested in your case. Someone on the staff of an established newspaper or well-known television news program would be best. The publicity might do you some good and would certainly help the cause of nonviolence.

Consider organizing a vigil at the draft board. Make sure to notify newspaper and television reporters in advance.

Your cause is right and your case is just. Make use of every legal right you have. Follow through with every step in the appeal process, regardless of how useless it may seem. This may be your best legal defense if the Selective Service ever takes you to court should all your efforts fail to secure CO status. Keep trying. There is an old Jewish and Jeffersonian belief that bears repeating here: The truth will prevail.

Bibliography

On Pacifism and Nonviolence

This abbreviated bibliography offers the names of general introductory sources. It omits specific works by and about the various apostles of nonviolence, such as Mohandas Gandhi, Henry David Thoreau, Leo Tolstoy, Dorothy Day, Cesar Chavez, Martin Buber, and Martin Luther King, Jr. Lengthier bibliographies on peace and nonviolence are available through CCCO, AFSC, FOR, and WRL.

Bondurant, Joan. *Conquest of Violence*. Rev. ed. Berkeley: University of California Press, 1965.

Brock, Peter. *Pacifism in Europe to 1914*. Princeton, N.J.: Princeton University Press, 1972.

———. *Pacifism in the United States*. Princeton, N.J.: Princeton University Press, 1968.

Bruyn, Severyn Ten Haut, and Paula M. Rayman. *Nonviolent Action and Social Change*. New York: Irvington Publishers, Halsted Press, 1979.

Camus, Albert. *Neither Victims Nor Executioners*. New York: Continuum 1980.

Chatfield, Charles. *Peace Movements in America*. New York: Schocken Books, 1973.

Cooney, Robert, and Helen Michalowski, eds. *The Power of the People*. Cooperatively and independently published by the editors (Palo Alto, Calif., 1977), with the help of Peace Press, Culver City, Calif., 1977.

Dellinger, Dave. *Revolutionary Nonviolence*. Garden City, N.Y.: Doubleday Anchor Books, 1971.

Finn, James, ed. *A Conflict of Loyalties*. New York: Pegasus, 1968.

————. *Protest: Pacifism and Politics.* New York: Vintage Books, 1968.

Gaylin, Willard. *In the Service of Their Country: War Resisters in Prison.* New York: Grossett & Dunlap, 1970.

Gregg, Richard B. *The Power of Nonviolence,* New York: Schocken Books, 1966. the classic text.

Guinan, Edward, ed. *Peace and Nonviolence,* New York: Paulist Press, 1973.
Basic writings by prophetic voices in the world religions.

Hallie, Philip. *Lest Innocent Blood Be Shed,* New York: Harper & Row, 1979.

Lakey, George. *A Manifesto for Nonviolent Action.* Chicago: Quadrangle Books, 1965.

Lorenz, Konrad. *On Aggression,* New York: Harcourt, Brace, Jovanovich, Inc.

Lynd, Staughton. *Nonviolence in America.* Indianapolis: Bobbs-Merrill, 1966.

McAllister, Pam, ed. *Reweaving the Web of Life.* Philadelphia: New Society Publishers, 1982.

Martin, David A. *Pacifism: An Historical and Sociological Study.* New York: Schocken Books, 1966.

Mayer, Peter, ed. *The Pacifist Conscience.* New York: Holt, Rinehart & Winston, 1966; Chicago: Regnery, 1967 (paperback).

Nathan, Otto, and Heinz Norden, eds. *Einstein on Peace* New York: Schocken Books, 1968 (paperback).

Nelson, John K. *The Peace Prophets.* Chapel Hill: University of North Carolina Press, 1967.

Pelton, Leroy H. *The Psychology of Nonviolence.* New York: Pergamon Press, 1974.

Schlissel, Lillian. *Conscience in America: A Documentary History of Conscientious Objection in America, 1957–1967.* New York: Dutton, 1968.

Sharp, Gene. *Exploring Nonviolent Alternatives.* Boston: Porter Sargent, 1970.

————. *The Politics of Nonviolent Action.* Boston: Porter Sargent, 1973.
One volume hardcover, three volumes paperback.

Sibley, Mulford Q. *The Obligation to Disobey: Conscience and the Law.* New York: Council on Religion and International Affairs, 1970.

————, ed. *The Quiet Battle.* Garden City, N.Y., 1963. Boston: Beacon, 1968 (paperback).
Writings on the theory and practice of nonviolent resistance.

────── and Philip E. Jacob. *Conscription of Conscience.* New York: Cornell University Press, 1952.

Stanford, Barbara, ed. *Peacemaking.* New York: Bantam Books, 1976.

Templin, Ralph T. *Democracy and Nonviolence.* Boston: Porter Sargent, 1965.

Weinberg, Arthur, and Lila Weinberg, eds. *Instead of Violence.* Boston: Beacon Press, 1965.

General Materials on Conscientious Objection and the Draft

Draft Counselor's Manual ($15.00).

Published by and available directly through NISBCO, this manual is indispensable, as are most of NISBCO's materials and publications.

CCCO's Draft Packet ($2.50).

Includes "Three Hundred Years: The Struggle for Conscience," "Conscience, War and the Selective Objector," "Is There a Draft in Your Future?", "So You'd Fight If . . .," "Are You a Conscientious Objector?", "To Study War No More" (a good bibliography), and CCCO's Registration Card for COs. Published by and available directly through CCCO, these are all indispensable, as are most of CCCO's materials and publications.

Seeley, Robert A. *Handbook for Conscientious Objectors.* 13th ed. April 1981.

Published by and available through CCCO. This is the newest in CCCO's succession of CO Handbooks. Like its predecessors, it is an invaluable guide.

Johnson, R. Charles. *Don't Sit in the Draft.* Occidental, Calif.: Nolo Press, 1980.

Pfeffer, Leo. *God, Caesar and the Constitution.* Boston: Beacon, 1975. See especially the chapter on "The Military"

Jewish Works

Much Jewish material is found in the first section of this bibliography, especially in the Finn, Mayer, and Weinberg volumes. Pay special attention to Buber's letter to Gandhi in the Mayer volume and the selections from Agrippa, Cronbach, Buber, Einstein, Stephen S. Wise, Freud, and Judah Magnes in the Weinberg volume. Also note the articles by Arthur Gilbert, Everett Gendler, Steven S. Schwarzschild, and Abraham Joshua Heschel in Finn's book *Protest* . . ., and to Gendler's excellent essay, "War and the Jewish Tradition," in Finn's other volume, *A Conflict of Loyalties*.

The Jewish Peace Fellowship has published a number of significant works. Try to locate back issues of JPF's magazines *Tidings* and *Shalom*, of blessed memory. Keep up with JPF's current quarterly newsletter *Shalom: The Jewish Peace Letter*, edited by Murray Polner and Carolyn Toll.

Three other works published by JPF that you should become familiar with are:

Can a Jew Be a Conscientious Objector? ($.05).

A short but incisive pamphlet, in a newly revised version.

Roots of Jewish Nonviolence ($1.00).

An instructive and indispensable paperback. Give special attention to Reuven Kimelman's "Nonviolence in the Talmud" and Everett Gendler's translation of the Aaron S. Tamaret essay "Passover and Nonviolence."

Shalom (available free).

A pamphlet furnishing the background, program, and philosophy of JPF. It also includes a membership form.

Several of the peace movements in Israel have published materials that are of vital interest to the would-be CO. Foremost among these, and constituting "must" reading no less than the publications of JPF, CCCO, and NISBCO, is the concise paperback, *Violence and the Value of Life in Jewish Tradition*. This all too brief but first-rate collection, edited and introduced by Yehezkel Landau, was published in 1984 by Oz Veshalom, the Orthodox peace movement, in Hebrew and English editions. Written from a progressive Orthodox perspective, it features superb essays by Immanuel Jakobovits, chief rabbi of Great Britain, Rabbi Emanuel Rackman, president of Bar-Ilan University, Professor Uriel Simon, and Rabbi David Shapiro. This volume is not to be missed. (The other Orthodox peace movement in Israel, Netivot Shalom, also publishes interesting and pertinent materials. Unfortunately, these have yet to be translated into English. Foremost among them for the Hebrew reader is *Torah, Tzionut, Shalom: Kovetz Ma'amarim* [Torah, Zionism, Peace: A collection of articles], which highlights, among others, an excellent essay by Ezra Fleischer.) Other illuminating Jewish works on our subject include:

Cronbach, Abraham. *Judaism for Today.* New York: Bookman Associates, 1954.

See the chapter "War and Peace."

Eisendrath, Maurice. "Sanctions for Peace in Judaism." In *World Religions and World Peace*, edited by Homer A. Jack. Boston: Beacon Press, 1968.

————. *Can Faith Survive?* New York: McGraw-Hill, 1964.

See the chapter "The Dilemma of a Pacifist."

Eliav, Arie L. *Shalom: Peace in Jewish Tradition.* Translated by Misha Louvish. Israel: Massadah Publications, 1977.

A beautifully illustrated and designed book offering an invaluable anthology of classical Jewish sources on the subject of peace. Compiled by one of Israel's preeminent political leaders and premier peace activists, this book is must reading in the original Hebrew or in this splendid translation.

Friedman, Maurice. *The Covenant of Peace: A Personal Witness.* Wallingford, Pa.: Pendle Hill.

————. "Hasidism and the Love of Enemies—A New Approach to Reconciliation." *Fellowship*, November 1964.

————. "Martin Buber and the Covenant of Peace." *Fellowship*, January 1966.

————. "Martin Buber and Pacifism." *Shalom* 17, no. 1 (Winter 1968).

Gendler, Everett. "Judaism and Conscientious Objection." *Response* 2, no 1 (Winter 1968).

Glatzer, Nahum. "The Concept of Peace in Classical Judaism." In *Der Friede: Idee Und Verwirklichung* (the Leschnitzer Festschrift). Heidelberg, 1961.

A superb and very important essay. This is "must" reading.

Greenberg, Irving. "Judaism and the Dilemmas of War—An Essay in Halachic Methodology." In *Judaism and World Peace: Focus Vietnam,* edited by Henry Siegman. New York: Synagogue Council of America, 1966.

Harlow, Jules. "Peace in Traditional Jewish Expression." In *Liturgical Foundations of Social Policy in Catholic and Jewish Tradition,* edited by Daniel F. Polish and Eugene J. Fischer. Notre Dame, Ind.: University of Notre Dame Press, 1983.

Jacobs, Louis. *Jewish Values.* London: Vallentine & Mitchell, 1960.

See the sections "The Love of Neighbor," "Compassion," and "Peace."

Korff, Samuel I. *A Responsum on Questions of Conscience.* Boston: Rabbinical Court of Justice of the Associated Synagogues of Massachusetts, 1970.

This fascinating responsum represents a disappearing genre—a rabbinic court's response to a moral and social issue.

Lelyveld, Arthur. "Jewish Imperatives and World Peace." In *Judaism and World Peace: Focus Vietnam,* edited by Henry Siegman. New York: Synagogue Council of America, 1966.

Magnes, Judah L. "Like All Nations?" In *The Zionist Idea,* edited by Arthur Hertzberg. New York: Meridian Books, 1960.

Montefiore, C., and H. Loewe. *A Rabbinic Anthology.* New York: Meridian Books, 1960 (first published, London: Macmillan, 1938.)

See the chapters "Peace," "Pity, Forgiveness and Love," "Divine Judgment, Divine Mercy," "Idolatry, Martyrdom," and "On Humility and Pride."

Neher, André. "Rabbinic Adumbrations of Nonviolence: Israel and Canaan." In *Studies in Rationalism, Judaism and Universalism in Memory of Leon Roth,* edited by Raphael Loewe. New York: Humanities, 1966.

An outstanding, scholarly essay.

Neusner, Jacob. "One Jewish Perspective on War." *Shalom* 17, no. 1 (Winter 1968).

Schwarzchild, Steven. "The Necessity of the Lonely Man." *Fellowship,* 1969.

Special consultation issue on "Moral and Technological Implications of Peace on Earth," (with comments by Arthur Cohen and Everett Gendler).

———. "The Religious Quest for Peace." *Judaism* 15, no. 4 (Fall 1966).

Tamaret, Aaron S. "Politics and Passion: An Inquiry into the Evils of Our Time." Translated by Everett Gendler. *Judaism* 12, no. 1 (Winter 1963).

An excellent, significant essay.

One pertinent and very moving novel that you will surely want to read is *The Last of the Just*, by André Schwarz-Bart (New York: Antheneum, 1960, paperback ed. 1973). Also read the discussion of Schwarz-Bart in James W. Douglass's fine book, *The Nonviolent Cross: A Theology of Revolution and Peace* (New York: Macmillan, 1966), pt. 2, chap. 60

Several of my articles might also be of interest to you. They reflect my perspectives as a Jewish peace activist on various dimensions of the Israeli-Arab conflict and of the Holocaust. These will be found in my book, *Meditations of a Maverick Rabbi: Selected Writings of Albert S. Axelrad*, Edited by Stephen J. Whitfield, with a preface by Nahum N. Glatzer (Chappaqua, N.Y.: Rossel Books, 1985).

It is strongly recommended that you acquire the sources mentioned in this bibliography, many of which are available in paperback, and develop your own personal library of peace literature. Aside from being a worthwhile end in itself, this will provide sources at hand for you to share with others, thereby strengthening your ability to serve as a peace messenger.

For a more comprehensive Jewish bibliography on Peace, Nonviolence and Judaism, contact the JPF.

Appendix

Introduction

On the following pages are excerpts from CO essays written over the years by various Jewish conscientious objectors. Most of the authors are now in the rabbinate, among the ranks of Jewish educators, or leaders in the Jewish community. Some were students of mine at Brandeis. Others sent me copies of their CO essays when it was publicized in Jewish magazines and in peace periodicals that I was writing this book. I am including these essays here for your own personal edification and to satisfy your sense of historical curiosity. You will probably find it interesting to read the words of your predecessors. I hope that you will benefit from their perspectives, but I also must caution you against copying them.

Several additional words of explanation are in order in connection with these essays. The first of them was authored by a man who was, at the time, a student at Harvard University. More recently, he made *aliyah* (moved to Israel permanently). From his home in Jerusalem, where he has become a distinguished leader in interfaith and peace work, he maintains his conscientious objection to war as an Israeli, as expressed in his recent letter to Gen. Ariel Sharon, then Israel's Minister of Defense, appended to his original CO essay.

Two of the other CO essays were composed by medical doctors, one of whom was actually in the U.S. Army at the time he wrote the essay. He was attempting to secure his release from the U.S. armed forces as a conscientious objector.

Finally, this section concludes with some rather moving and

pertinent material, starting with the selection "When War Comes," written between the years 1938 and 1949, but mostly during World War II, by Rabbi Stanley Brav, then of Cincinnati, Ohio. Though it is not, as such, a CO essay, it would appear to be of interest and relevance to the reader. The very last piece in the Appendix is also the most recent, the 1985 draft resistance statement of Andy Mager, a courageous declaration of conscientious refusal rooted in Judaism.

Selection I

ANSWERS TO SSS FORM 150

Series I—Claim for Exemption

I am, by reason of my religious training and belief, conscientiously opposed to participation in war in any form and I am further conscientiously opposed to participation in noncombatant training and service in the Armed Forces. I, therefore, claim exemption from both combatant and noncombatant training and service in the Armed Forces, but am prepared to perform civilian alternative service if called.
(Statement B on SSS Form 150)

Series II—Religious Training and Belief

1) Describe the nature of your belief which is the basis of your claim and state why you consider it to be based on religious training and belief.

My religious opposition to warfare, and to my participation in it, is based on my faith in both the righteousness and the effectiveness of human love (interpersonal compassion), which I consider the highest Good. I firmly believe that a "good" end or objective is one that furthers the purpose of man's existence. I hold, on religious faith stemming from my belief in God, that man does have a Divine purpose for his earthly existence (a destiny or mission), and, moreover, that all men's souls or consciousnesses are embodied for the same ultimate purpose. After having identified this preliminary religious position, I am now trying to define just what that purpose is, or at least what *my* earthly mission might and should be. I sincerely believe that my Divine essence would be furthered most by the enrichment of human lives through the unfolding of my love. This belief is the product of all my religious and spiritual training, outlined below. And as I search for righteous and self-fulfilling tasks for myself, I am also defining actions that are, for me, morally reprehensible and ultimately self-defeating (or Self-defeating). Such an immoral action is engaging in warfare, in any capacity. Since this judgment is based on my conception of the meaning of goodness, and since that conception is derived directly from my religious convictions, I feel I can validly claim that my refusal to participate in warfare is based on my religious training and belief.

2) Explain how, when and from whom or from what source you received the religious training and acquired the religious belief which is the basis of your claim. (Include here, where applicable, such information as religion of parents and other members of family; childhood religious training; religious and general education; experiences at school and college; organizational memberships and affiliations; books and other readings which influenced you; association with clergymen, teachers, advisers or other individuals which affected you; and any other material which will help give the local board the fullest possible picture of how your beliefs developed.)

The growth of my religious/moral convictions is probably as complex a process of spiritual development as any and is not completely accountable in retrospect. But I shall attempt to outline my religious training and the evolution of my thinking as thoroughly as I can.

My immediate family subscribes to Liberal Reform Judaism and belongs to Temple Beth El in Spring Valley, New York. All my formal religious training has been at that temple, from Sunday and Hebrew Schools, through Bar Mitzvah training, and beyond to further study of Judaism and other religions in preparation for my Confirmation at the age of fifteen.

Throughout most of my youth, I absorbed without full appreciation or understanding the profound lessons of Jewish teachings and Jewish history.

I do remember, however (even today), a magnificent small book called *Let's Talk about Right and Wrong* (written by Dorothy Kripke), which I read during my early years in religious school. It espoused brotherhood, interpersonal respect, and compassion for others. And to a small boy who had yet to encounter the harsh realities of intergroup and international prejudices, the book offered a noble ideal: the equality and dignity of all men.

My subsequent Jewish education was neither rigorous nor inspirational enough to make of me a traditionally devout Jew (in the ritualistic sense), but it provided what I am certain is the foundation for my current religious convictions. I have always admired and appreciated the intellectual freedom, the absence of theological dogma, inherent in Judaism. In fact, my mind was so free of doctrinaire theology that I was able to combine, for a time, a religious skepticism with a secular and academic interest in natural science. But even as I developed the self-image of an agnostic biochemist, the social consciousness and concern of Jewish ethics had won, in me, a sincere and active adherent. By the time I was Bar Mitzvah at thirteen, I was just about old enough to understand what the Hebrew word "mitzvah" really means. The literal translation is "commandment"; and as I became a "son of the commandment" (Bar Mitzvah), I could recognize and accept the moral responsibilities that I was assuming in entering into a personal covenant with God.

I did not study the Scriptures intently, so few passages come to mind offhand. One that has always stood out, though, is Isaiah's famous prophecy of swords, plowshares, spears, and pruning-hooks. Another is this passage from Malachi: "Have we not all one Father? /Hath not one God created us? /Why do we deal treacherously every man against his brother,/ Profaning the covenant of our fathers?" And in the prayer book my congregation has used, one prayer has similarly caught my solemn admiration. It begins: "Grant us peace, Thy most precious gift . . ."

When I graduated from high school in 1967, I was anticipating an educational program and career in biochemistry. But for as long as I can remember I have been as much a humanist as I was then a natural scientist. At my commencement exercises I delivered an address, which, I feel, evidenced my humanism and foretold the changes that my mind and plans would undergo within a year. In that address I spoke of the choices before mankind: annihilation or world-building. I discussed the widening gap between man's technological expertise and his social wisdom, and I proposed education as the most promising means of narrowing that gap and averting the final and irrevocable catastrophe.

My freshman year at Harvard College saw a major change in my general thinking about life and its meaning. I registered with Local Board 13 in September, 1967, and considered seriously the conscientious objection question at that time. But I could not then find in my conscience the strength and clarity of conviction necessary to declare as a conscientious objector. At Harvard I spent a great amount of time in classes and laboratories but still had ample time to think about nonacademic matters. What I thought about most was the bigotry and mental anguish of some close friends at college. I could not understand their minds and realized that there was so much about human behavior and attitude development that I did not comprehend. And meanwhile I mixed chemicals.

My non-science courses and professors proved to be more interesting in my freshman year than my sessions with test tubes and slide rule. I took a social science course bearing the simple title, "War." It was taught by a brilliant and inspirational political scientist, Stanley Hoffmann. As a study in history, government, and ethics, the course confirmed my belief in the ultimate futility of international conflict, no matter how "just" the political motives proclaimed. But another course taken that year was the most valuable of all those I have yet encountered at Harvard. It was the philosophy course in ethics which I enrolled in for the spring term of 1968. It was a well-constructed course with a wide range of readings, from Plato to contemporary discussions of civil disobedience. The professor, Roderick Firth, was quietly engrossing. He suggested rather than preached, and despite all his apparent wisdom his act of intellectual offering was strikingly humble. Although the course was certainly informative and influential in itself, its great value lay in the time to think which it provided me.

As mid-term approached, I spent three weeks preparing for the term paper due in my ethics course. Dissatisfied with the several definitions of "goodness" that had been presented to me by moral philosophers, I tried to formulate my own definition. In the course of that mental search, I underwent an identity crisis and spiritual conversion simultaneously and quite suddenly. In one sleepless night all the pieces of my life and my morality came together. In a flash of creative discovery (was it insight? revelation? fantasy?) I conceived of my "human essence" theory of the meaning of goodness, holding that goodness is synonymous with the furthering of man's existential purpose, his essence. I use the label "spiritual conversion" to describe this insightful process because it was far more than a merely intellectual awakening for me. Concurrently with my moment of moral insight I sensed the supernatural existence of a Divine Being or Force responsible for my own existence. I felt then, and still feel, that my consciousness or soul was embodied for a Divine reason and that it is my formidable task to discern that purpose.

I believed in God for the first time.

In formulating an ethical position consistent with this religious base, I quite naturally drew from my Jewish training and ideals. Fortunately, I had fallen in love the previous summer and was able to recognize the mystical wonder and joy, the self-fulfillment, and the social benefits of that supreme state of existence. (I believe in a Supreme Being and in supreme being, and my spiritual quest is now directed toward determining more precisely a personally valid conception of each.) I came to see love as the spiritual force at the heart of my Divine essence, and I perceived my life-long mission to be a constant effort to help build a world in which love among men is the guiding force in interpersonal and intergroup relations. I decided to leave biochemistry and major in social relations, in preparation for a career in education. (My courses last year and this year, along with my teaching experiences, have affirmed the rightness of that decision.) As my own contribution to a world of peace, I shall try to aid the interpersonal development of children and guide them to social awareness and concern in a loving way. I view my educational career as the major component of a life-style devoted to effecting constructive social changes. It is a socially activist career; and, I feel, it demonstrates my continual efforts to combine social action with religious and moral concern (which was Gandhi's great accomplishment). My social consciousness is definitely one vital product of my Jewish background.

Just as I acknowledge my obligation to serve others, I recognize my great debt to my country. I believe that my life-style and my objectives demonstrate a sincere patriotism and love of my country. My country is not just an expanse of land under a flag; it is millions of people with problems and hope. I want to help solve those problems and realize those hopes. I made another important resolution in mid-March of 1968; because my love for humanity is inseparable from my love and devotion for my country and its ideals, my conscience will not permit me to serve in her Armed Forces; and I must seek a 1-O classification. I am firmly convinced that the surrender of one's moral options into the hands of a state (particularly in times of war, with the personal subscription to a national policy of mass murder and destruction) is never justifiable, even in a case of national self-defense. I refuse to be trained to kill, injure, and destroy; and, as I explain below, I further refuse to enter the Armed Forces in a noncombatant capacity and execute orders which contribute to an immoral enterprise. All these activities I consider personally immoral because they contradict the essence of my humanity *and* the humanity of others—that common humanity which we all must recognize as sacred. My whole life-style is based on service to humanity, including service to my country in constructive ways.

Since the time I developed this position, I have encountered thinkers who have strengthened my convictions by their similar arguments and by their exemplary righteous actions. Martin Buber, the great Jewish philosopher, is one; Gandhi, another; and Martin Luther King, Jr., yet a third. I have reread Scriptural passages with new insight and have drawn spiritual strength from them also. And I have related more intensely to the moral ideals of Judaism, becoming a more conscientious Jew. I joined the Jewish Peace Fellowship and the Fellowship of Reconciliation in August of 1968 to affiliate myself with organized efforts to promote peace and understanding through compassion and justice. I can honestly state that my convictions are my own, freely and often painfully arrived at, and that they are sincerely held. It is on the basis of these religious and moral convictions that I seek a 1-O classification as a conscientious objector. I refuse to participate in war in any form, with the phrase "in any form" applied equally to "participate" and to "war."

3) To what extent does your religious training and belief restrict you from ministering to the sick and injured, either civilian or military, or from serving in the Armed Forces as a noncombatant without weapons?

My religious/moral convictions would not restrict me in any way from assisting sick or injured persons, whether soldiers or civilians, providing I was a civilian myself. I would consider such service highly commendable, and I have no objection to fulfilling my alternative service in such a civilian capacity. However, I must, by virtue of my beliefs, refuse to serve as a noncombatant soldier, in such a medical capacity or any similar assignment. By joining the Armed Forces I would surrender my cherished religious and ethical freedom. Even as a noncombatant medic, I would be subject to orders from superiors that could endanger, through my instructed behavior, the lives and well-being of human beings—either "friendly" troops and civilians or those deemed "enemies" by my government. On a more general level, consonant with the Nuremberg Principles, I refuse to affiliate myself with any organized effort whose objectives entail murder, destruction, or intimidation. My conscience does not allow me to fulfill my obligations to my country in such an immoral enterprise. I agree completely with Harvard Professor George Wald: man's business, and certainly mine, should be with life and growth, not with death and destruction.

4) Have you ever given expression publicly or privately, written or oral, to the views herein expressed as the basis for your claim? Give examples.

I have on many occasions during the past year and a half spoken to friends of my religious convictions and of the course of action which they demand of me. I have discussed my views with my college roommates [names and hometowns cited]. I have discussed my position with counselors and advisors, including my rabbi, Louis Frishman, Rabbis Milton Weinberg (Pearl River, New York), Albert Axelrad (Brandeis University), and Michael Robinson (Croton-on-Hudson, New York and Chairman of the Jewish Peace Fellowship), JPF member Jeremy Kagan, FOR youth director Ron Young, and FOR counselor Rick Lasky.

In addition, I have expressed my religious views and my attitudes concerning human affairs in writing and in public. Certainly, in joining the Fellowship of Reconciliation and the Jewish Peace Fellowship I proclaimed publicly my determination to promote peace through reconciliation. The most pertinent *written* expressions of my views are two essays: (1) "The Human Essence Theory of the Meaning of Goodness," written in March of 1968 for Philosophy 16 at Harvard College, Roderick Firth, Professor, and John Troyer, section leader; and (2)

"Utopian Education and the Destiny of Man," written in May of 1969 for Social Relations 98 at Harvard, Dr. Rose Olver of Amherst, Massachusetts, seminar director. I feel that my valedictory address before the Class of 1967 at Spring Valley Senior High School (entitled "Mankind: The Coming of Age" and delivered in June, 1967) also demonstrates my apprehensive concern with man's social problems and my faith in the socially therapeutic power of education.

I should also like to cite my recent activities and actions which, I feel, most clearly indicate the sincerity of my convictions by representing efforts to achieve reconciliation among groups and to promote peace and understanding—in my community, in America, and in the world at large:

(a) Teaching activities among economically underprivileged children . . . 1) Head Start program, Spring Valley, summer of 1965; 2) recreation program with predominantly black youngsters, summer of 1968, operated under the auspices of Ramapo Central School District #2 by Dr. Earl Nissen and Mr. Al Smith; 3) as a teacher's aide at the New School for Children in Boston, academic years 1968–69 and 1969–70.

(b) Political activity . . . 1) as founder and leader of the interracial Youth Alliance for Community Action in Spring Valley, New York, working to pass the Ramapo 2 school budget in July of 1968, in the belief that a defeat would lead to interracial antagonisms and conflict in my community; the enclosed position statement, which I drafted, explains why I was so concerned and why I worked strenuously to see the budget passed; 2) as an active campaigner for two politicians whose commitment to peace and to a sensible and humane American foreign policy merited my wholehearted support: in the summer of 1968 I worked for the primary victory of convention delegates pledged to Senator Eugene McCarthy, thereby continuing efforts on Senator McCarthy's behalf begun at Harvard that spring; in Spring Valley I worked out of the Concerned Democrats' office, operated by Mr. Leonard Leonetti and others; in that primary campaign I was a district co-ordinator and door-to-door canvasser in two Ramapo township election districts. After the New York primary and the Democratic National Convention, I concentrated my efforts on the re-election campaign of Congressman John Dow (27th C.D.), joining Young People for Dow in Rockland County and then, after my return to Harvard in September, the Committee for a New Politics (which raised funds for congressional candidates, such as Mr. Dow, who advocated an end to the war in Vietnam). I attended rallies and speak-outs, including the mass rally at the Boston Garden in late October of 1968 (entitled "Eleven Votes for Peace" and featuring Senator McCarthy, Paul O'Dwyer, and John Gilligan as speakers).

That is my record to date, gentlemen. Of course, it is only the beginning, the beginning of a life aimed at promoting peace and harmony among persons and groups—through teaching, through political action, through loving/living every day of my life.

[Years later . . .]

Fast of Gedalia 5743
20 September 1982

Minister of Defense Ariel Sharon
Israel Defense Ministry
Tel Aviv

Dear Mr. Defense Minister:

At the outset of the new year, I extend my best wishes for a year of peace and prosperity to you, your family, and all *Am Yisrael* [the Jewish People].

I regret having to bother you with a personal problem at such a difficult time, when you are busy attending to much more important matters. I am addressing my request to you because, under Israeli law (*Hok Sherut Bitachon*, 1959, paragraph 28c), you are the one authorized to resolve matters of this sort. And the problem arises now because I have been called by *lishkat hagiyus* [the office of conscription] in Jerusalem to appear this Wednesday, 22 September, for "clarification and registration."

I am a religious Zionist who has made *aliyah* from the United States out of an identification with Israel and the Jewish People. My professional background encompasses the fields of psychology, comparative religion, and education. I left my nuclear family and a promising academic career in America in order to live and work in Israel. My particular problem arises from the fact that I have always been, and still am, a conscientious objector to military service in *any* army. Being a Zionist and a C.O. creates an obvious inner conflict of loyalties. *I appeal to you to help me resolve it by allowing me to serve our country in the sherut leumi* [national service] *framework* available to religiously observant women. I want to offer my services to Israel in the same degree expected of any soldier my age, including the equivalent in time of yearly *miluim* [Reserves] duty. I am prepared to serve in any social or educational field where I am needed. And during wartime, I would certainly do whatever task I am assigned to help the civilian population, or wounded soldiers in a hospital, within any framework outside *Zahal* [the Israel Defense Forces].

My position as a conscientious objector predates by many years my coming to Israel in 1978. My C.O. convictions are religious, not political—they do not derive from the policies of this or any other Israeli government. As proof of my longstanding adherence to these convictions, I have attached two supporting letters which date from 1969, when I was preparing my C.O. case to present before my American draft board. One letter is from my U.S. Congressman, the other from my high school principal. Additional letters, from Israelis who have come to know me, are also appended to substantiate my present request for alternative, nonmilitary service.

Clearly it is more difficult to be a C.O. in Israel than it is anywhere else, since we are confronted by adversaries who seek Israel's destruction. The natural question that arises is the one which *Moshe Rabbeinu* [Moses, our teacher] already posed to the tribes of Reuven and Gad (*Bamidbar* [Numbers] 32:6)— "Shall your brethren go to war and you will sit here?" I have wrestled with this question for years. It weighs heavily and constantly on my conscience, and it compels me to prove that my principles are not just a cover for ethical egotism. In defense of my *personal* position, I cite, within our Biblical tradition, the example of the Levites. For that tribe had its own model of national service, also called *"tzava"* [army] in *Bemidbar* 4:3, which exempted the Levites from the national military census. They had a spiritual function (*avodat avodah*), along with physical burdens (*avodat masah*), which were assigned to them by the Torah and were kept distinct from the military service and burden assumed by the other tribes. Within this general division of national duties, I identify with the Levites. I see my work as an essentially religious task that aims at healing the social relations between Jews and non-Jews, both in Israel and abroad. The way my character and conscience have been molded, I simply could not reconcile within myself that basic life-task and the role of the soldier. I would be so spiritually and psychologically torn that I would be unable to function in either capacity, if I were compelled to undertake both.

I worked for two years on the staff of the Israel Interfaith Association; I am active in the International Council of Christians and Jews; I presently teach at Nes Ammim, the Christian village in the Galilee; and I am working on several writing projects, including a book I am co-editing for Paulist Press in New York on the role of Israel in Jewish-Christian relations.

Through my teaching at Nes Ammim, and my contacts with visiting Christian and interfaith groups, I have many opportunities to advance Israel's cause through *hasbarah* [interpretation, explanation]. I do the same during my work-related trips abroad. In defending, before non-Israelis, the right of Israel to defend herself against attack, *I never raise the issue* of my personal inability to accept army service. My C.O. convictions are a strictly private matter which I do not broadcast to others. I deeply respect the sense of duty which most Israelis feel in fulfilling their national service through *Zahal*. And I realize that without our army, Israel would not exist as a free and independent nation.

My Zionist beliefs led me to make *aliyah* and apply my interfaith training here in Israel. If I were not a Zionist, I could easily avoid the whole issue of military service in other ways. I could, of course, return to the United States, but I choose to make my home here. I could resume full-time yeshiva study, but I can not, in good conscience, use that framework to escape my social responsiblities. Of course, if I were a woman, I would have the simplest option of all: declaring myself either a member of a religious family or someone who can not serve in the army for "reasons of conscience" (ta'amim shebematzpun). Under Israeli law, both of these religious groups, women and yeshiva students, are exempted altogether from army duty *without* being required to do alternative national service. My own conscience dictates that, if I request and receive a personal exemption on religious grounds, then I am morally obligated to do some alternative *sherut leumi*, which I will gladly do.

I would be happy to meet with you to discuss my case, when you are not so preoccupied with national problems that demand your daily attention. I have cancelled my participation in an international interfaith conference next month, to which I was invited, in order to be available to meet with you and anyone else whose jurisdiction touches on my request.

Once again, I convey my wishes for a pleasant new year and a *gamar chatimah tovah*.

Since having submitted this letter, Yehezkel Landau has reached a mutually-satisfactory understanding with Israeli army, which allows him to fulfill his annual reserve duty in the Civil Defense branch of the military rather than in a combat unit.—A.S.A.

Yours sincerely,

/s/ Yehezkel Landau

Selection II

1. I consider my beliefs to be based on my religious training, and consequently hold the following principles. I believe that committing murder for any reason is a sin against God. My religion teaches me that if one's enemy does one harm, one must not retaliate with harm, but rather attempt to thwart any harm through love. I have been taught that because all men are created by God, no man can say he is better than another, thus has no right to take another's life. If one were to take the life of another, he has shown judgment over the man by deeming him unfit to live, which is the only human reason for murder. No man has the right to this power to judge others: this power truly resides only in God. My religion teaches me that man must be more concerned with not injuring others rather than being careful not to be injured. Those that are careful not to injure others reinforce the existence of the God of Truth and Justice and add power to His kingdom, yet by ignoring this wisdom and killing, one shows that one is more concerned with his own welfare, which detracts from the power of the kingdom of God and denies His existence. This is going against the commandment "that ye remember the day of your departure from Egypt all the days of your life," which means that the Jews must remember that their power lies in the God of Truth and Justice who brought them to freedom from their oppressors in Egypt. I have learned that man must reject bloodshed and violence altogether, and in this way help mankind further approach goodness in the eyes of God. This is not to say that one who refuses to accept violence does not suffer. Man

consciously suffers by setting his soul against the strong, which opposes the concept that he passively submits to the will of the evil-doer. In this sense, one who refuses violence stores a powerful weapon. In these ways committing violence denies the existence of God and the basic beliefs of my religion.

2. My beliefs will not permit me to serve as a noncombatant in the Armed Forces. I do not oppose helping human beings who are injured or sick, because I feel it is the duty of a man to do his best to help those less fortunate than he. Yet if I were to aid the injured while serving in the Armed Forces, I would be accepting its principles of violence. In this way, I would be strengthening the power and principles of the Armed Forces. Because I cannot go against the principles of my religion, I do not wish to be a helpful factor within and to the Armed Forces, though in a purely civilian capacity I would help any human being, including, of course, soldiers.

3. Throughout my entire life I have had close contact with my temple. I have been mostly influenced by my parents who have brought my brothers and I up in a religious home, primarily teaching us the importance of knowledge and respect for our religion. After moving to Needham eighteen years ago, my parents assembled with several other Jewish parents to raise money for a temple in Needham. Eleven years ago, the temple was finally constructed, and a religious school established. While attending religious school, my parents played vital roles in the leadership of the temple. My mother has been a sisterhood member and has served as vice president and president in the course of her involvement. My father, a board member and brotherhood member, has served as president of the brotherhood and president of the temple. My parents' dedication towards our temple has greatly affected my brothers and me. My older brother and I became b'nai-mitzvah and confirmed by Rabbi Kaplan, who has had a great influence on me. My younger brother, having recently become a bar-mitzvah, will be confirmed in three years. During my years in high school, I was involved in our temple youth group, which is a chapter of New England Federation of Temple Youth. During

these three years I had an active part in this organization which instructed the teachings of Judaism to teenage youth. The youth group gave me an opportunity to come into contact with many of the finest and most respected Rabbis in this part of the country. I attended two conclaves with about one hundred other selected youth members. These conclaves, each under the direction of about ten rabbis, taught me much about our religion. One of the conclaves' themes was "Violence and Judaism," which greatly influenced my ideas on the issue of violence and my religion. It was these conclaves that inspired me to become more active in our Temple Youth Group, and become chairman of the Programming Committee in my junior year and Vice President of the youth group in my senior year. My close affiliation with our youth group advisor, with our current Rabbi, Rieven Slavkin, and the members of the group had a tremendous effect on my contact with my religion. As a student at Brandeis University, my religion has become an important part of my education, this being the only Jewish sponsored university in the country, with one of the finest schools for Judaic studies in the country. At the present time I am taking a course dealing with the Bible, taught by a very well known and respected professor of Jewish studies, Dr. Nahum Glatzer.

It has been through close association with the Temple, NFTY, and my present studies at school which have served as vital contributors to my religious training.

4. The clearest example showing that my beliefs are deeply held is the fact that I do not and never had participated in any violent or aggressive action causing physical harm to anyone or anything. I cannot condone physical violence as a means of solving disagreements of any kind. Therefore, I cannot force myself to inflict physical harm, because, in so doing, I feel it would be against the principles of my religion.

5. My beliefs affect the way I live as a sincere supporter of my religion. Seeking to enter some field that will be socially beneficial, I am seriously considering studying law. This profession would enable me to help solve problems encountered

personally between men and to promote the importance of justice and truth in our society. During nonworking hours, I plan to continue my involvement in the temple that I belong to, carrying a leadership position while participating in the temple functions. Because I consider my religion a vital part of my life, I am constantly studying its teachings and principles, and how they interact with problems in our society. I hope that my religious education will always serve to direct my actions and ideas towards justice in the eyes of God so that I may consider myself to be a positive influence to humanity.

6. I have often expressed my beliefs publicly in the past. Many of my ideas have been expressed in my youth group, where discussion groups were major functions of the conclaves and conclavettes. Outside of the Youth Group, I have discussed my opinions with teachers and students at school. Since my opposition is not politically based, I have not participated in anti-war rallies, which serve to raise only political opposition to the principles which I oppose, but the basic individual religious beliefs which I am concerned with upholding. For these reasons, my expression has been restricted to private surroundings. Among these, one of most recent sounding boards and resource persons has been Rabbi Albert S. Axelrad.

Selection III

1.Describe the nature of your belief which is the basis of your claim and state why you consider it to be based on religious training and belief.

I am opposed to participation in war in any form by reason of my belief in the value of a Jewish way of life, by reason of my belief in the sanctity of life, and by reason of my subsequent commitment to constantly affirm the sanctity of life by seeking peace through peaceful means. Conflict can never be reconciled by war, but only through dialogue in which each side affirms the basic humanity of the other; therefore I find myself committed to search for peace through dialogue and not through aiding the maintenance of a balance of military terror.

The Bible tells us that man was created in the image of God which is merely a way of saying that man partakes of the Divine Essence. This is what makes each human life an individual of unsurpassable value. This Ultimate Value of Life in and of itself is the dominating factor which must be recognized above all political, sociological, and psychological considerations of how I must govern my behavior.

The implication of this belief in relation to my participation in war is clear. Man partakes of the Divine Essence, thus to do injustice to man is to do injustice to the Divine Presence within man. War is nothing less than the most atrocious injustice which can be committed against man and it is therefore the ultimate injustice against God, the ultimate blasphemy. Modern warfare depreciates not only the lives of soldiers, but also the lives of civilians and this depreciation can not be tolerated if one wishes to avoid doing injustice to man and ultimately to God.

The belief that I as a Jew should be committed to work for peace is found among the most fundamental teachings of the Bible. In the Book of Deuteronomy (30:19-20), God spoke to the Children of Israel and said:

> I have set before you life and death, blessing and curse; therefore choose life that you and your descendants may live, loving the Lord your God, obeying His voice, and cleaving to Him; for that means life to you, and length of days.

This appears to be a direct exhortation for the man who desires life to live in the way of God, to settle disputes not by violence, but through understanding of the problems at hand. This idea is also expressed in Leviticus Rabbah 35:5:

> The sword and the Book were bound together and sent upon the earth. God said: If you adhere to the Book you will be saved from the sword; if not, the sword will destroy you.

More recently this view has been expounded by Martin Buber, the Jewish philosopher who was in his time a leader in seeking Arab-Israeli reconciliation. In his work Buber stressed the importance of the development of I-Thou relationships between men as opposed to the development of I-It relationships. Basically what this means is that each person should be considered as an entity valuable in his own right and not as an object to be manipulated or used. In dealing with one with whom there is a disagreement the proper thing to do is to affirm the humanity of the person and his right to partake of a just solution to the problem, and not to deny his humanity as is done in war. This means that one does not destroy the enemy, but on the other hand one invites him into one's home so that a peaceful solution may be found. The efficiency of this method may be seen in relation to Buber's own life. When during the early days of the Arab-Israeli conflict the Arabs attacked the border town in which Buber lived, Buber fled the town. The

Arabs destroyed all the property in the section where Buber had lived and had been writing, but they left Buber's house standing, thinking that he might still be inside hiding.

Peace is not a mere dream or something which is only to be prayed for, but it is something which we must work and struggle for. The stress on doing what is right and working towards peace is found at the basis of Jewish thought, and is echoed in the words of Henry Slonimsky, former dean of Jewish Institute of Religion. Slonimsky says that the essence of true religion is "to insist on God in a Godforsaken world, or rather in a world not yet dominated by God, and thus call Him into being." —Henry Slonimsky, *Essays* (Cincinnati: Hebrew Union College Press, 1967), p. 127.

Although Slonimsky was not an Orthodox Jew, his thoughts seem to resemble those of the traditional viewpoint:

> To think nobly and to desire goodness—this is not the ultimate attainment. To act nobly and to do good, stands higher. To think and to act nobly, to desire and to do good, and not to allow any gap to separate the harmonious entity which is man, approximates perfection. Torah, teaches us the road, the Halachah, to this perfection. Man will become better only by better deeds; only by the nobility of his conduct will he become truly ennobled. Without the ma'ase ha-mitzvoth, the actual performance of its commands, Torah and man will remain unfulfilled.
>
> —from "Faith and Observance" by Dr. S. Weiss in *What Is Orthodox Judaism*, published by Union of Orthodox Jewish Congregations of America, p. 21.

It is in accordance with this tradition that I have chosen to live my life.

There is violence in the world, there is suffering in the world, wars are still being fought, and probably will be fought in the future. I can not ignore these things, neither can I condone them by becoming a part of the military machine which helps to perpetuate them. We pay men to make guns and pay others not to produce food because of misplaced values and perverted priorities. My opposition to participation in the armed forces is based on my unwillingness to have my religious values destroyed, or my sense of priorities altered from what I know is right. I shall continue to use the Torah as a guide for the way I am to live my life.

2. Explain how, when, and from whom or from what source you acquired the religious training and belief which is the basis of your claim.

The process by which I acquired my present beliefs is rather complicated. I come from a Jewish family and attended Hebrew School in an Orthodox synagogue, Fleetwood Synagogue, Mt. Vernon, N.Y. This gave me a religious grounding in Judaism which I have not forgotten, but which for a time ceased to be an integral part of my belief system. In 1966 my family moved to Danbury and I found myself in an environment in which I found that Judaism was more of a social than a religious organization. I became disillusioned with Judaism and for a time became rather confused as to religious matters. During this time I began to study other religions and Oriental philosophy to see how these compared with Judaism.

When I entered Brandeis University in 1968 I was registered as a Physics major. At Brandeis I was confronted with social and religious problems which I had not encountered before. I found that I had only a vague notion of how I was going to live my life, and that Physics was not relevant to the problems I was really concerned with (e.g., myself, other people, religion, politics). I changed my major to Psychology at the end of my freshman year hoping to gain a better understanding of people and the causes of conflict between them.

During my second year at Brandeis I became a regular attendant at Havurah, a group of people who come together on the eve of each Sabbath in an effort to find expression for their Jewishness. I found that Judaism could provide a form for the way life should be lived. I began to examine different philosophies of Judaism, Orthodox, Reform, and Reconstructionist, and to evaluate their meaning and relevance for me. I was aided in this by Rabbi A. Axelrad. I read widely and changed my religious practices at various times to see what was best. Among the books I have read and which have influenced my thought are the Bible; *Israel and the World* and *I and Thou* by Martin Buber; *Essays*, Henry Slonimsky; *The Judaic Tradition*, Nahum, Glatzer; *Foundations of the Metaphysics of Morals*, E. Kant; *Sanity and Survival*, Jerome Frank; *A Guide to Jewish Knowledge*, Chaim Pearl and Reuben Brookes; *On the Duty of Civil Disobedience*, Henry David Thoreau; *Ethics of the Fathers (Pirke Abot)*; and *What Is Orthodox Judaism*, UOJC. I found that each philosophy had its good points and its bad points; I tried to take the best points of each. My present religious philosophy lies somewhere between the Orthodox and Reconstructionist points of view. The great emphasis on law and Torah of the former, and the emphasis on Jewish peoplehood of the latter are both part of my belief.

While my commitment to work for peace has been established for some time (see question 4), my opposition to participation in war arose only as a result of more prolonged study and consideration of how I was to live my life. A person can be Jewish and still not be truly religious. I have decided after careful consideration that I can not be at peace with myself unless I am religious—in the words of Slonimsky, unless I "insist on God." I have added to my commitment to work for peace a commitment to lead a religious life. These two commitments taken together mean, as I have already shown in my answer to the first question, that I can not participate in any way in the Armed Forces of the United States.

3. To what extent does your religious training and belief restrict you from ministering to the sick and injured, either civilian or military, or from serving in the Armed Forces as a noncombatant without weapons?

It is the purpose of the medical corps or any other noncombatant branch of the Armed Forces to aid in the successful completion of the destructive tasks of the Armed Forces. This is illustrated by the following statement from the Army Field Manual FM 8-10 (p. 195).

> The primary duty of the medical troops as of all other troops is to contribute their utmost to the success of the command of which the medical service is a part.

As a civilian I would not hesitate to aid anyone who was sick or injured, but as a noncombatant in the Armed Forces I would still be giving my support to that institution (the Armed Forces), an institution whose values are the antithesis of the values by which I try to live my life. For this reason I find it impossible to serve in any branch of the Armed Forces.

4. Have you ever given expression publicly or privately, written or oral, to the views herein expressed as the basis for your claim? Give examples.

My commitment to work for peace and to reconcile conflict through dialogue manifested itself during my first year at Brandeis. In January, 1969 a group of Black students took over a building on the Brandeis campus and issued a list of non-negotiable demands. In an effort to resolve the conflict before violence occurred I joined a group of four other students and one faculty member. This group worked out a plan which was instrumental in opening communication between the Blacks and the Brandeis administration. Enclosed is a letter of appreciation for my efforts signed by the former President of the University, Morris Abram.

Also during my freshman year at Brandeis I wrote a letter to the Dean of Faculty at Brandeis concerning an opportunity to work on a special committee. In this letter I expressed my commitment to work for peace and a better world. A copy of this letter is enclosed along with the response of the Dean.

I have enclosed copies of two papers written for a philosophy course I took last year (1969-1970) at Brandeis. The paper on Kant might be said to establish a philosophical justification for leading a religious life. The paper on Machiavelli reflects my views on war. These papers reflect the development of my thinking during my sophomore year at Brandeis.

My commitment has led me to participate in several peace demonstrations and a recent religious service on behalf of Soviet Jews.

My religious beliefs find frequent expression in my participation in Havurah which meets weekly on the Sabbath in celebration of the Day of Peace.

My refusal to participate in war, as I have said above, resulted from my decision to add to my commitment to work for peace a resolution to lead a religious life. This resolution may be said to have grown from the thoughts expressed in the documents presented here as well as from the sources referred to in question 2. I have spoken of this frequently with Rabbi Axelrad and with a close friend, Nancy Forse. Less frequently I have spoken to Alan Shapiro, a friend from Mt. Vernon, who was instrumental in introducing me to Orthodox Judaism when I was younger. I have not had an opportunity to write about my resolution to be religious; being religious is something one must do, not something one must write or talk about.

Selection IV

BELIEFS WHICH ARE THE BASIS FOR MY CLAIM FOR
CLASSIFICATION AS A CONSCIENTIOUS OBJECTOR—AND
WHY THESE BELIEFS WOULD NOT PERMIT ME TO SERVE
IN A NONCOMBATANT POSITION IN THE ARMED FORCES

I am conscientiously opposed to war. My belief in God and my love of life would never allow me to kill a person.

I am Jewish. The Jewish religion, its teachings and its traditions represent the foundation of my belief and the basis for my nonviolent feelings and ideals. Since early childhood, I have been influenced by the Bible and by the heritage of eternal and universal peace taught by Jewish sages. The most important ideal for me comes from the Commandment, "Thou shall not kill." Killing for me is the worst sin that one can commit. My conscience would give me no peace if I were ordered to kill or even trained to kill.

The foundation of Jewish life has survived for thousands of years because of its belief in peace and nonviolence. "Love thy fellow man," the ancient Jewish spiritual leader Hillel taught, because it is the "kernel of the entire Jewish teaching." I will always believe that God's most precious gift to the world was life and the basic teachings of Deuteronomy echo this: "I call heaven and earth to witness against you this day, that I have set before thee life and death, the blessing and the curse, therefore choose life, that thou mayest live, thou and thy seed."

My belief in nonviolence has always been extremely important to me and I have always tried to preserve life. I have tried to help people who are hurting emotionally and physically. I have helped to raise money for people who suffer from serious diseases. I have raised pets such as dogs, hamsters and guinea pigs. I have never consciously killed or injured insects or any other living creatures.

My beliefs would not permit me to participate in any war or serve in the military in any capacity. I could never use or fire a weapon of any kind. Nor could I serve in good conscience in a noncombatant position in the military. I could not serve as a noncombatant, i.e. medic, because in my heart I would feel as if I were participating in war as much as the person who actually fights. Therefore, my moral and religious beliefs in nonviolence bring me to the decision of seeking Conscientious Objector, 1-O status, should I ever be classified.

How I Acquired These Beliefs

I began to acquire my beliefs and attitudes about nonviolence while I was still a child.

During the late 1960's, my parents participated in peaceful demonstrations against the Vietnam War and they brought me on marches in New York City. The war was the major topic of discussion in our house. Although I did not understand the complete significance of every aspect of it, it was during this period of my life that I began to realize that I was opposed to fighting and to violence. It was the beginning of my belief in pacifism.

My parents are both Jewish and I have been raised in a Jewish household. When I was eleven, I asked my parents if I could attend a synagogue religious school. They were more than happy that I was reaching out for a Jewish education and gladly consented. It was at this time that my family—my parents, my brother and my sister—joined Temple Isaiah of Great Neck, New York. And it was at this point in my life that my formal knowledge of Jewish tradition, history, heritage and law began.

My family had sometimes attended Jewish Sabbath services before I began religious school. And some Judaic customs had always been observed in our home. Now, Jewish ritual and custom became a *major* part of our family's everyday lives. We began celebrating all of the Jewish high holy days and all other Jewish holidays at the temple. We began our tradition of celebrating the Sabbath every Friday evening with prayer and the traditional Jewish meal. Whatever our various schedules during the rest of the week, all five of us try to be home on Friday evenings and all of us say the blessings. We regularly attend Friday services at the temple. I am frequently called upon to help lead the service.

My parents believe that I have changed the way our family lives and thinks. (My mother became chairperson of the temple's religious school and my father became a trustee of the temple.) With the inspirational teachings of our rabbi, Harold Spivack, my comprehension of the Jewish religion was enriched and many of its peaceful and nonviolent attitudes were further instilled in me. I became Bar-Mitzvah after my formal Jewish training at age thirteen and then made a long awaited trip to Israel to witness first-hand the roots of my ancestry and heritage.

As I reached manhood, I joined the temple's youth group, where I absorbed many new ideas and started making decisions and forming opinions on my own. The discussions of the youth group and the talks over dinners at home stimulated my intense feelings about peace and this in turn made it easier to cope with the problems and conflicts of the world.

July 1979 marked a major turning point in my life. My father had frequently talked to me about peace and war, conscientious objection and choices. Dr. Murray Polner, vice president of the Jewish Peace Fellowship, was a name often mentioned during our family discussions and I decided that I wanted to meet him to talk about peace, war, the Jewish tradition and conscientious objection. I went with my father to see Dr. Polner and we spoke for many hours with him and his son, also a conscientious objector. After I left the Polner home I decided to go on record as a conscientious objector.

I joined two organizations dedicated to peace and nonviolence: The Jewish Peace Fellowship (JPF) and the Fellowship of Reconciliation (FOR). I have filed a statement of my beliefs with the Central Committee for Conscientious Objectors (CCCO) in Philadelphia and with the National Interreligious Service Board for Conscientious Objectors (NISBCO) in Washington, D.C.

My intellectual growth was rapid after that. I began reading books, articles and pamphlets on violence, nonviolence, war and pacifism. Two books particularly influenced me: *The Economy of Death* by Richard J. Barnet provided me with an insight into the futility of war, especially nuclear war, and war's enormous cost in lives and waste. Michael Herr's book, *Dispatches*, painted the horrifying picture of Vietnam from the point of view of the American foot soldier. Of the many pamphlets which have influenced me, "Roots of Jewish Nonviolence," "Conscientious Objection and You," and "Are you a Conscientious Objector?" were particularly important for their facts and views.

Many important ideas were expanding and developing in my mind as I increased my reading and began to enter into more discussions. I followed and read more closely about violence and controversy in the world. Through magazines, newspapers and television, I read and listened for views on nonviolence. Many of these ideas have become an essential part of my beliefs.

I feel that my parents have been the most important influence in my life. They have always respected my opinions and have encouraged me to pursue as much knowledge on any subject as possible. Nonviolence has always been an important part of their lives and they became conscientious objectors at the same time that I did.

As I continue to grow, and acquire ever-deeper beliefs in peace through nonviolence, I will hopefully be able to convey my feelings to other people and live a life free from war. In the words of the Bible, "In tranquility and trust shall be my strength."

How These Beliefs Affect the Way I Live, and the Type of Work I Plan to Do

Becoming a conscientious objector was the most important decision of my life.

At age sixteen, I filed a registration card with the Central Committee for Conscientious Objectors. After taking this step I spent countless days thinking and writing my answers (contained here) to questions asked on "Worksheet on War" provided by NISBCO. I have done this well in advance of a possible call by the Selective Service to register for the draft or to be classified. I have established conscientious objector files with the Jewish Peace Fellowship and the Fellowship of Reconciliation in Nyack, New York, NISBCO and CCCO. These files contain letters from teachers, friends and my rabbi attesting to the sincerity of my beliefs in peace and nonviolence—beliefs which for me had their beginnings many years ago when I was still a child.

I continue to conduct my life by this credo: With the choice of the direction in which he may go, man can guide his own destiny. The freedom of thought and choice determines the type of man one is and it is in deeds that he becomes aware of what his life really is, of his power to harm and to hurt, to build and to create.

I apply my nonviolent attitudes to the way I relate to people through work and play. For example, in the summer of 1980, I was a counselor at a day camp. My job was to plan and organize activities for sixty young children. To run the program harmoniously, I frequently called upon the philosophy of Mahatma Gandhi: "Nonviolence is not a cover for cowardice but it is the supreme virtue of the brave." Thus, instead of allowing the children to tear each other apart with their fist fights I showed them how to settle differences peacefully by talking out their problems. I know from letters that they wrote to me after camp that they had a wonderful and healthy time.

Throughout my life I have avoided violent confrontations,

simply by not fighting. I chose instead to discuss and to argue issues. As I have grown older, I have tried to work out potentially violent situations and bad feelings through reconciliation. I have spent hours at meetings, debates and rallies, listening and talking to people who favor war as a viable solution to conflict and to those who oppose it. I have seen that discussion can narrow differences if given the chance.

For me, long distance running has provided a nonviolent, noncontact outlet. Here, the individual is faced with a one-to-one relationship: The mind and the body. For me, long distance running, as a sport and an outlet, again evokes the teachings of Gandhi: The nonviolent person offers resistence "only in moral terms. He states his readiness to prove his sincerity by his own suffering rather than by imposing suffering on the assailant through violence. Cowardice is wholly inconsistent with nonviolence . . . nonviolence presupposes the ability to strike."

I practice my belief in nonviolence in other public ways. I have marched in rallies in New York City to support the peaceful emigration of Jews from the Soviet Union. I have participated in peaceful anti-war marches. I discuss peace and war with friends and with those who are not yet my friends. I believe with Rabbi Everett E. Gendler that "Direct communication must not cease among men, however greatly they may differ in outlook."

As for future occupations, my beliefs would prevent me from working in any job where I might be required to cause death or injury to another living thing. I could not work in a defense plant, a nuclear missile factory or a slaughter house. Because I could not carry a gun, I could not become a policeman. For the same reason I could never be a hunter even for sport.

The beauty of the world and the contrast between the serenity of nature and the inhumanity of some human beings has led me to seek an area of employment in which I can create peaceful environments in the world. I have chosen political science.

It seems to me that an understanding of politics and the

history of governments, war and peace, can provide a means of bringing about urgent but peaceful change in the world.

The study of political science will provide me with an historic basis for discussion, debate and necessary peaceful compromise. Political science is a field in which I feel that I can work peacefully and nonviolently. It is a future to which I eagerly look forward.

Selection V

"Describe the nature of your belief which is the basis of your claim and state why you consider it to be based on religious training and belief."

My opposition to war in any form stems from my identification with the teachings of Judaism as they have developed over the past 4000 years and from my interpretation of the meaning of this long history.

Furthermore, my beliefs encompass not only war in any form, but any situation in which I may be called upon to shed the blood of one of my fellow men.

The reasons for this belief I can trace to the source of all Western religious thought—the Bible, and also in other Jewish sources.

First of all, *human life is sanctified.* "God created man in His own image . . . Male and female created He them." (Genesis 1:27) This statement is *not qualified in any way.* It does not refer to Jews or Catholics or Americans or Vietnamese or Koreans or Germans. It says "man" and that means *all of mankind.*

Furthermore, the same book of Genesis states that man has *the capacity to know the difference between good and evil (3:22) and, therefore, he is held responsible for his actions with regard to his brothers, not just for his own self-interests. (4:9)*

Indeed, the story of Cain and Abel is an excellent example of my point. Cain slew his brother Abel out of envy. God certainly had the power to slay Cain in punishment, but He did not. God is all-powerful, but He is also the highest example of "Rachamim," mercy. Thus, not only did He spare Cain from death, but He put a mark on him so that others would not slay him.

The image of "Hàel Harachaman," the God of mercy, runs through-out Jewish tradition and history. He is always seen in the final analysis as "the Merciful One," and "full of loving-kindness."

For example, on Yom Kippur, the Day of Atonement, which is the example par excellence of God's mercy, we find Jews all over the world reciting prayers such as "For all of these, O God of forgiveness, forgive us, pardon us, grant us atonment," and "For we do not present our supplications before Thee for our righteous deeds, but because of Thy great mercies. O Lord, hear; O Lord, forgive; O Lord, harken and deal kindly with us."

God's mercy and forgiveness is not unqualified, however. The most important teaching of Yom Kippur is not to pray only to God for forgiveness, but that if one has sinned against his fellow man, he must first do all he can to right the wrong before God will forgive him.

"Repentance on the Day of Atonement only secures forgiveness for transgressions against God; as for example, when one has partaken of forbidden food or indulged in illicit intercourse, and so forth. But transgressions against one's fellow-men, as for instance, if one wounds, curses or robs his neighbor or commits similar wrongs, are never pardoned till the injured party has received the compensation due him and has also been appeased. Even though he has made the compensation, the wrongdoer must also appease the one he has injured and ask him forgive-ness. Even if a person only annoyed another in words, he has to pacify the latter and entreat him till he has obtained his forgive-ness." (Maimonides, *The Book of Knowledge*, Laws of Repentance, chapter 2: 9; XI–XII)

If we return to the Bible, we can see that there are many examples of this teaching. The writers of the Bible were espe-cially fond of showing how the different nations of the world are descended from various parts of the families of the patriarchs—Abraham, Isaac, and Jacob. There are many instances in which there are problems between these people; however, the story of Cain and Abel is one of the very few cases in the Torah (Five Books of Moses) in which violence was used.

Examples of the opposite solution which was greatly preferred are Abraham and Lot, Abraham and the three strangers, Jacob and Esau, and Joseph meeting his brothers when they came to Egypt.

Looking at two of these we can see what this preferred solution was.

The story of Jacob and Esau has always impressed me greatly. The two were twins with very different temperaments. In addition, they had an ongoing quarrel over the birthright, which, we are told, was stolen away from Esau by Jacob's trickery. This quarrel, however, never came to open battle, though Jacob was constantly afraid that his brother would kill him.

In Genesis Chapter 33, Jacob encountered Esau with four hundred men. Preparing for the worst, Jacob went forth to meet his brother, but they did not fight. Instead, "Esau ran to meet him, and embraced him, and fell on his neck, and kissed him; and they wept." (Genesis 33:4)

In the example of Abraham and Lot, the solution is less emotional and more rational. Abraham simply said to Lot, "Let there be no strife, I pray thee, between me and thee, and between my herdmen and thy herdmen; for we are brethren. Is not the whole land before thee? Separate thyself, I pray thee, from me; if thou wilt take the left hand, then I will go to the right; or if thou take the right hand, then I will go to the left." (Gen. 13:8–9)

This, of course, was not an easy choice for Abraham, because Lot would obviously take the better portion; however, the maintenance of their good relations and the prevention of strife were the overriding factors in Abraham's decision.

Thus, the Torah teaches us that all peoples and nations are our brothers, and that peace is possible if we really desire it. If we insist on preserving only our own selfish interests, however, violence will be the inevitable result.

Coupled with this in my conviction that war is not a viable solution is the *ultimate commandment of God*—"*Thou shalt not murder.*" (Exodus 20:13, Deut. 5:17) Not only is it stated twice, but it is unequivocally direct. There are no qualifications. I must interpret this as a direct commandment from God to me and every other human being not to kill any other person. Thus, I must expand the definition of murder, in this sense, to include any situation, *including war*, in which one person deliberately kills his fellow.

The reason for this interpretation which I have made is that *God is the ultimate in both power and mercy. Only He has the right to take human life, since He created it. And if, in His mercy, He has even once refused to do so, how much more so am I forbidden to do so under any circumstances.* Moreover, I can not aid or assist another person or organization to perform such a deed. Instead, I must strive for the solutions of Abraham and Jacob, not of Cain.

This interpretation is not only mine. The Talmud, in which are recorded the discussions of the ancient rabbis on the laws of the Torah, says, "in every other law of the Torah, if a man is commanded 'transgress and suffer not death' he may transgress and suffer not death, excepting idolatry, incest, and shedding blood . . . Murder may not be practised to save one's life."

There are, of course, many examples of war in the Bible. However, none of them change the case. Only if the war is between the Jewish people and Amalek, or one of a very few other peoples, is one compelled to participate. The fact is, however, that these peoples no longer exist, so there can never be a war in which one must fight, and the rabbis were very quick to point this out.

Secondly, war exists in the Bible, but it is clearly not the ideal. The great fathers of the Jewish people, as I have shone, made every effort to avoid conflict.

The kings of the first and second commonwealths waged wars; however, let us examine the situations closely.

David was a great warrior. He slew Goliath when he was only a boy, and fought both with and against the Philistines. What he is remembered for in Jewish tradition, however, is not his might. He was the great king who played the lyre sweetly to soothe Saul, and composed the Psalms. David wanted to build the Temple to God; however, God specifically refused him, because he was a "man of war." This honor was delegated to Solomon, the king of peace, prosperity and commerce, who was blessed with great wisdom to solve conflicts peacefully.

The prophets always made the distinction between the present, which was never good enough (and still is not) and the ideal which they said would eventually come. This is what Isaiah was referring to when he said:

> "And it shall come to pass in the end of days, that the mountain of the Lord's house shall be established as the top of the mountains, and shall be exalted above the hills; and all nations shall go unto it. And many peoples shall go and say: Come ye, and let us go up to the mountain of the Lord, to the house of the God of Jacob; And He will teach us of His ways, and we will walk in His paths. For out of Zion shall go forth the law, and the word of the Lord from Jerusalem. And He shall judge between the nations, and shall decide for many peoples;
> And they shall beat their swords into ploughshares, and their spears into pruning-hooks; Nation shall not lift up sword against nation, neither shall they learn war any more." (Isaiah 2:2–4)

This theme of the Messianic age is adumbrated by all of the prophets. Not one of them, however, ever said that it will come of itself. It will only come when all men fulfill the commandments of God concerning righteousness and fair dealings with one's fellow men who are in need. Thus, Jeremiah said:

> "Execute ye justice and righteousness, and deliver the spoiled out of the hand of the oppressor, and do no wrong, do no violence to the stranger, the fatherless, nor the widow, neither shed innocent blood in this place. For if ye do this thing indeed, than shall there enter in by the gates of this house kings sitting on the throne of David . . ." (Jeremiah 22:3–4)

Thus, with regard to war, the theme in the tradition which seems to me to be the most important is summarized in the Psalms:

"Depart from evil, and do good;
Seek peace and pursue it." (Psalm 34:15)

This and the commandment not to kill are the most important for me in the Jewish tradition. Indeed, as Hillel, a contemporary of Jesus said, "What is hateful unto thee, do not do unto thy neighbor. The rest is all interpretation."

In summary, the core of my claim as a conscientious objector is the sanctity of human life, the brotherhood of all men, the imperative to find the non-violent solution, the prohibition of killing a human being, the necessity of doing justly, and the admonition to "seek peace and pursue it."

Thus, I must declare that on the basis of this religious belief which I have been trained in and firmly believe, I can never participate in war in any form. For, as the Talmud says:

"Anyone who takes a life, it is written of him in the scriptures, it is as if he killed a whole world. Anyone who saves a life, it is written of him in the scriptures, it is as if he saved a whole world."

(Mishna Sanhedrin 37)

Question #2

"Explain how, when and from whom or from what source you received the religious training and acquired the religious belief which is the basis of your claim. (Include here, where applicable, such information as religion of parents and other members of family; childhood religious training; religious and general education; experiences at school and college; organizational memberships and affiliations; books and other readings which have influenced you; association with clergymen, teachers, advisors or other individuals which affected you; and any other material which will help give the local board the fullest possible picture of how your beliefs developed.)"

The earliest and most basic influence on my religious and ethical makeup has been my family. My father, who is a reform rabbi, has always placed great emphasis on my education, awareness of moral and ethical values and the choices which they entail, and a cohesiveness of the family unit.

This last point is where I think I ought to begin. As far back as I can remember, our family has always been close. We say the "Hamotzi" prayer before each meal. Every member of the family has always been expected to participate. Also, the Shabbat (Sabbath) has always held a special value for our family. At Friday night dinner my mother lights the Shabbat candles and we all recite together the blessings over the candles, the wine, and the bread, and then wish each other Shabbat Shalom—Sabbath Peace. This phrase, I feel, has become an integral part of my personality—Sabbath Peace and Blessing.

Following the meal we again say a prayer to thank God for providing for all of our needs, after which we read from the Torah (Five Books of Moses) and my father gives an explanation of the passage, usually including a story from the Jewish tradition having a moral point. The family ceremony is concluded with singing, following which we all usually go to Friday evening Shabbat services together.

Saturday has always been "family day" during which, whatever we decide to do, we do together as a family. These activities are not necessarily religious in nature, but the total effect is to make the day special, because it is the Shabbat and we are a Jewish family.

The most beautiful part of the Shabbat for me, especially as I recall impressions as a little boy, is the ceremony of "Havdalah" (separation) on Saturday evening, separating the Shabbat from the rest of the week. This ceremony involves lighting a candle with six wicks to symbolize the week, and then saying prayers over the candle, and the wine and a spice box, to symbolize the sweetness of life and the week to come, and then dousing the candle in the wine to end the Shabbat. We traditionally follow this with the song "Shavuah Tov," a "Good Week" which goes, in translation:

> "A good week,
> A week of peace,

May gladness reign
And joy increase."

The Shabbat is important in the development of my personality and temperament, I feel, because of the pervasive mood of
calm, peace and togetherness with my family.

An additional aspect of the cohesiveness of my family which
I feel is important is that whenever there is an argument, my
parents call us together for a family meeting in which we sit
down, and sometimes rationally, sometimes rather emotionally, discuss the problems and try to come to an acceptable
compromise. The responsibility of each member of the family
to do his share of the work, and to take his share of the
responsibility is always paramount. It is because of the influence of this aspect of my background, I feel, that I have always
held rational discussion and compromise to be, by far, the best
method of dealing with problems. It has taught me, in addition, that the other person's opinion is something to be respected.

The second issue which my parents have always stressed
greatly is education, both secular and religious. Especially with
regard to Judaism, my father has always taught me that I must
be an "informed-participating-Jew." By this he means, it seems
to me, that as a Jew I have a two-fold responsibility; to know
the sources of my heritage and its contents, and to practice
them as I believe that they should be practiced. Above all, no
decision may be made out of ignorance. I must know, especially, what is morally and ethically expected of me, and make
my decisions on the basis of my own knowledge and judge-
ment.

I can remember one particular instance of this teaching of my
father's which occurred when I was about fifteen years old. It
had to do with sexual and moral conduct. He said that I must
make the decision for myself what kind of life I want to live.
Nobody can make that decision for me.

With regard to decision-making, there is a point which he
has made many times, namely, that I must first decide what it
is that I have to do, then determine what the alternatives are

for achieving it, and then choose one that I feel is the best and do it. This, I feel, is one of the most important things that he has ever taught me.

Since, as I have said, no decision can be made out of ignorance, my education has been quite extensive. When I was very young, I studied Hebrew and my Jewish heritage with my father. Many of the stories which we read, or which he told me, have to do with the great rabbis of ancient times, all of whom prized study and learning both as an end in itself, and as a tool for living a rich and fulfilling life.

I also attended religious school where my father was the rabbi from 1953 to 1966. In 1963 I was Bar Mitzvah, at which time I ritually became a full-fledged member of the Jewish community, taking on both the responsibilities and the privileges which that entails.

In 1964 I was confirmed, graduating from the religious school. The subjects of discussion in the confirmation class, extending over a two year period, were interfaith cooperation and understanding, and also a study of the processes by which Reform Judaism developed as an attempt to make Judaism meet the needs of Jews living in the modern world, faced with modern problems and situations. This whole process further impressed me with the value of rational thought and action as a means of solving problems.

I have also been greatly influenced in this regard by my mother. For many years she has been active in the community on the issue of civil rights. She was a member, and for a while the chairman of, the Human Rights Commission, appointed by the city council in our midwestern city.

While we lived there, my mother worked on her master's degree in sociology. Her thesis was on the reactions of the Black communities of this country to White efforts to equalize housing facilities.

Since we moved to Massachusetts, my mother has taken the job of Executive Director of Community Relations Council.

The effect of my mother's interests on me over a great portion of my life has been, again, to instill within me a respect for rational solutions to problems, and above all, avoiding violent solutions.

Until my senior year in high school, however, my experience as an independent person practicing the principles which I have learned was very limited. I cannot say that I was an extremely aware person, probably due to the fact that I was rather shy.

The first semester of my senior year in high school, however, proved to be one of the greatest turning points in my life. I spent that semester as a member of the Eisendrath International Exchange program to Israel (sponsored by the National Federation of Temple Youth, of which I was a member), living with an Israeli family in the city of Haifa, and attending classes at the Leo Baeck High School.

In order to go on this program, I had to first master a considerable amount of Hebrew, over and above what I had already studied with my father, and in the community Hebrew school. I studied for about five hours a day from the time that school got out in the Spring until I left in July.

My strongest and most lasting impression of Israel was that there I was in a country where there are Jews from all over the world. They are all different in many respects, but the overriding fact remains—we are all Jews.

This was not just an ideological feeling which was indoctrinated into me. While I was in Israel I lived with two very different families. One was originally from Austria and Germany, and the other came from Poland. In addition, I met Jews from many other parts of the world, such as Yemen, India, North Africa, England, etc. What impressed me was the ideology that we have a common bond as Jews which had become a reality for me. I also realized, of course, that ideology is as powerful a force of separation and alienation as it is of identification: however, I was most impressed with the feeling of unity.

While I was in Israel I began to study Jewish history and literature in a way I never had before. Together with the other members of the exchange program and Rabbi Robert Samuels of the Leo Baeck School, we explored the literary records of the suffering and joy of our people through the centuries, and the events which led up to the founding of the state of Israel.

One story which we read which particularly impressed me was "The Three Gifts" by Y. L. Peretz. This story points out both the mercy of God, and the highest moral and ethical standards which are expected of every person.

Upon returning to the United States I continued my study of Hebrew literature and Jewish history. Already the idea was forming within me that I wanted to become a rabbi.

During the summer of 1966 I was a member of the National Torah Corps of the National Federation of Temple Youth, the same organization which sponsors the exchange program in which I had participated the summer before. The National Torah Corps is an intensive seven week program of study in Hebrew and Judaica, in which young people from all over North America participate.

The atmosphere of this program, I feel, is especially important for my claim, because in the intensive setting of a summer camp institute personal tensions and conflicts are bound to come out. Keeping Peretz's story in mind, however, I tried to deal with each person according to the highest moral and ethical values.

This was augmented by my study during the course of the program, of the "Pirkei Avot," the "Ethics of the Fathers," and the book of Jeremiah under the guidance of Rabbi Shai Shaknay, a very warm and likeable person, who, unfortunately, recently died of cancer at a very untimely age. Many of the passages which I quoted in answer to the first question of this form I first studied and discussed with Rabbi Shaknay during that summer. Especially the "Ethics of the Fathers" became for me not only a purely academic exercise, but also a model by which I must guide the moral and ethical decisions which I must make in my life, always striving for the highest possible level of awareness and conduct.

In addition, under the guidance of Alan Smith, at that time a student rabbi at the Hebrew Union College–Jewish Institute of

Religion in New York City, I studied modern Hebrew poetry and prose. It was with him that I encountered again, the first time having been in Israel with Rabbi Samuels, a poem by C. N. Bialik, the national poet of Israel, entitled "If You Would Like to Know." (Translation attached for your reference) This poem had not originally made a great impression on me; however, upon rereading it in the summer of 1966, I was struck by the philosophy behind it. It has to do with why the Jewish people have been able to survive millennia of persecution and poverty without succumbing. The answer, Bialik says, is in the Old Synagogue and the study of the Torah (law), at once the refuge and the delight of the Jewish people over the centuries. The devotion to God, even under such horrible conditions is the most important and beautiful part of Jewish history. Never once did the people lose their faith in God's mercy, or in the importance of their responsibility to know and live by His laws and commandments.

Bialik does say, of course, that what is left in the Old Synagogue is only a remnant spark. However, where there is the spark of life, there is infinite hope. Where that spark is extinguished, there is no hope.

Upon entering Brandeis University in the fall of 1966, I had decided, I thought, that my goal was to go into the rabbinate. I therefore enrolled in courses in Judaic studies and Hebrew. As a consequence of my studies during that year, and subsequent events which I will explain, I have decided that my calling does not lie in the rabbinate. I still remain dedicated to the principles of my religion, however, and accept the fact that I must take a significant amount of responsibility and leadership in the Jewish community anyway.

It was during this first year in college that I turned eighteen and registered with the Selective Service. I did not sign series VIII of the classification questionnaire at that time because, although I feel now that the content of my background at that time was sufficient for me to have been a conscientious objector, I did not know anything about conscientious objection from a legal point of view, and also, I was not faced at that time with the necessity of making an immediate choice as to whether I would or would not serve in the Armed Forces. My beliefs have certainly crystallized greatly since then; however, this crystallization has been the result of and in response to concrete situations and demands on me to make decisions of a moral nature. As I have said, I have always been taught and firmly believe that all decisions of this nature are strictly up to me to make, and, furthermore, must be made both from a position of knowledge and from a confronting of the specific issues involved. The war in Viet Nam, as you can, no doubt, surmise, has had a great deal to do with the crystallization of my position with regard to all wars. I could not make the decision in a void. I have always had a distaste for violence as a means for achieving anything, but in opposing war I must make my decision existentially, that is, in response to the situations as I encounter them.

Thus, I did not choose to file as a conscientious objector at that time, but instead, accepted a II-S student deferment.

During the summer of 1967 I was on the staff of the Union Institute of the Union of American Hebrew Congregations in Oconomowoc, Wisconsin, as a counselor, Hebrew teacher, and music teacher in their "Pioneer Camp," a program very similar to the National Torah Corps in Warwick, New York, in which I had participated the summer before.

There were a number of student rabbis on the staff there, and I had many lengthy discussions with them on Jewish history, ethics, Zionism, etc. In addition, the tenor of the "Pioneer Camp" program was Zionistic, thus reviving in me the feelings which I had first felt during my stay in Israel about the unity of the Jewish people, and, as an extension of that, the unity of all mankind.

I had heard many stories about the Israeli War of Independence and the Sinai Campaign of 1956, and of the heroism of the Israelis. Trying to put myself in their position, however, I could not even force myself to accept the premise that war could be justified, because I had seen the cemetery on Mount

Herzl outside of Jerusalem for those killed in these wars, and the waste of human life and potential appalled me.

Returning to Brandeis in the fall, I decided that, although I still felt that I wanted to go into the rabbinate, I should get as broad an education as possible, so I switched my major from Judaic studies to history.

During that year I taught a post-confirmation class at Temple Reyim in West Newton, Massachusetts. In this class I discussed with teenagers between the ages of thirteen and fifteen issues such as the war in Viet Nam, drugs on the college campus and in the high schools, sexual morality in today's world, and theology for the Twentieth Century.

It was during that year that the war in Viet Nam became more and more of a real issue for me, as I was forced to confront body counts in the newspapers, political battles over strategy, and the whole moral question of war in discussions with my friends and teachers. Also, I began to realize that if I have a real position against war, then it is my responsibility to declare it. (As I look back on it now, I can see how I was influenced by what my father had taught me, namely to act on my decisions.) I still did not declare myself as a C.O., however, because I was still unclear as to what it really entails.

During the second semester of my sophomore year at Brandeis, I applied to the Jacob Hiatt Institute, a one semester study program in Jerusalem sponsored by Brandeis. I was accepted and left in July, 1968 for my second extended stay in Israel.

The intervening three years had done much to quell the enthusiasm which I had felt about Israel while I was on the exchange program, and coupled with my increased maturity, I was able to take a more critical view of what I found there.

First of all, another war had been fought since my previous visit. Certainly I had been concerned in June of 1967 about the survival of Israel because of my friends and relatives there, and because of my feeling of unity with all Jews, wherever they are. The recourse to war, however, and the Israelis' justification—"Ayn Brera," "There is no choice," disturbs me greatly. Following the most recent war, there has been a tremendous increase in the amount and quality of justification of war on the part of the Israelis. Although, in a sense, I can see how they have been frustrated by twenty years of continued bloodshed, and the repeated failure of attempts at negotiation, this reaction, it seems to me, blinds them to the fact that war only leads to repeated war. The only permanent solution can be in the foundation of a mutual trust by both sides and a willingness to make concessions which may not seem to be immediately advantageous, or even detrimental in the immediate perspective, but which will display more clearly than words ever could the good will and desire for peace. Furthermore, I believe that it is up to Israel, as a Jewish nation to initiate this trust.

Thus, as I have said, I was faced with a greatly changed country on my second visit. The first person I met when I arrived in Jerusalem was a twenty-five year old woman named Yael Chen, one of the advisors for the institute, who had been married for two years before her husband was killed in the Six-Day War. I was impressed by her bravery in dealing with her tragedy; however, over the six months in which I came to know her, I was greatly distressed by the chaos into which her emotional being had been thrown. I had never before encountered in such a personal way what war does to people, and it horrified me. I came to the conclusion that the price of her husband's life could not possibly justify the capture of the Old City of Jerusalem (in which he was killed). Ideology leads to a refusal to compromise, and it is this lack of willingness to compromise both on the part of the Israelis and the Arabs, as well as on the part of the United States and the Soviet Union which has given rise to the conflict in the Middle East, and in many other parts of the world. What right can any government have to destroy the infinite potential of even one human life?

As I toured the territories conquered by Israel from the Arabs in 1967, I could not shake away the feeling that it is all so senseless. My enthusiasm of 1965 was badly disillusioned.

There are several other specific incidents which occurred

while I was in Israel which I feel are relevant to the crystallization of my position.

At one point it was arranged for the members of the institute to travel to the city of Nazareth to meet with some Christian Arabs. We were divided up among several families for dinner.

When I arrived at the home of the family with whom I was to have dinner, I was struck by their situation. They live in what amounts to a mansion by Israeli standards. They were all very polite, and the younger members of the family spoke excellent English and Hebrew, although the older ones only spoke Arabic, so that my conversation with them was limited, since I do not know any Arabic.

When the conversation turned to politics they assured me that they want very much to be loyal Israeli citizens; however, the Israeli government has a covert policy of suspicion of even the most respectable Arabs living in that country. Until just before the 1967 war, they were not allowed to leave Nazareth without a special travel permit, even though, many residents of Nazareth (all Arab) work in the port city of Haifa, about a half hour away by bus.

They do not support the Arab members of the Jewish parties because these people they consider to be puppets. Their only alternative is the Arab Communist Party, which most of them vote for even though they are not really communists.

Many Israeli Jews, including some of my closest friends, had warned me not to believe a word of what any Arab might tell me, and justifying this warning with the statement, "Well, you don't know the Arab mentality like I do. They'll serve you with one hand and stab you in the back with the other." I could not help but believe the sincerity of these Arabs. I felt, however, that if their desire for equality is further denied, that they will eventually turn on the Jews of Israel just as the Blacks are turning on the Whites in this country. Violence, I must once again point out, results from an inability to compromise on the essential platform of mutual trust. What better place can there be to begin a solution than to trust? Otherwise there is no hope. A military victory only leads to bitterness and renewed violence. Thus, I could only see the wasted potential for friendship and cooperation with these Arabs.

The second incident which influenced me greatly, and also upset me quite a bit, was when I went to the exhibition of the Israelis Armed Forces in Tel Aviv with my cousin, who is the principal of an elementary school in Ramat Gan, a suburb of Tel Aviv. The exhibition was of the history of the Israeli Armed Forces, their present armaments and accomplishments, and also a display of Soviet equipment captured from the Egyptians and Syrians during the most recent war.

I was very much upset by the overt militarism of Israeli society which such an exhibition displays, and the increase in such militarism due to the glorifying of the army by such an exhibition. My cousin, who is a very mild mannered person, and would not lift a finger against any one, became very upset at my remarks. She said that I just do not understand. That to be a pacifist in the United States where we are safe from direct attack is one thing, but that Israel cannot afford such things.

My reply is quite simple. My cousin, and most Israelis may think that it is necessary for Israel to have a strong army, but I do not agree. The army must not be glorified, furthermore, because to do so is to glorify warmaking. Also, to glorify the army means that one can very easily lose sight of the fact, as most Israelis have done, that peace, not military victory is the goal, and that ultimately peace will not be won by the army. It will be won by the good will of the people, and their implicit trust, and the good faith in which negotiations are undertaken. This is what I have learned from my studies of history and my own personal observations in the world in which I live.

Thus, as I returned to the United States, it was with a greatly increased sense of urgency about the whole political situation in the world. I came to the realization that the teachings of Judaism which have been instilled within me are not mere abstractions. They are imperatives for action.

There is a passage from the Talmud commenting on the

passage from the Psalms—"seek peace and pursue it" which says:

> "The Torah does not command you to run after or to pursue the other commandments, but only to fulfill them upon the appropriate occasion. But peace, you must seek in your own place and pursue it even to another place as well." (Leviticus Rabba, Tzav IX, 9; Numbers Rabba, Hukkat XIX, 27)

I was still not in a position to declare the fact of my objection to war on my return, however, because I still did not know enough about the legal details. But I had made up my mind that I would do so as soon as I could.

While I was inquiring into the possibilities of my becoming a C.O., I was also switching my major at Brandeis from History to Psychology. I had finally come to the realization that I did not really want to be a rabbi. I still accept the imperative, however, to be an "informed-participating-Jew," and my desire to work directly with people is no less than it ever was. I am planning to study for a Ph.D. in educational psychology after I graduate from Brandeis in June, 1970.

In my study of psychology, I have been exposed to several theories which have influenced my thinking and actions. The most important of these is the writings of Erich Fromm in his books *Escape From Freedom, The Sane Society, Man for Himself,* and *The Art of Loving.*

According to Fromm there is an ideal personality type which he calls the "productive personality." No person is this personality type, but all people are closer or farther away from it.

Fromm defines productiveness as "an attitude which every human being is capable of, unless he is emotionally and mentally crippled." (*Man for Himself,* page 97). Such a person, it seems to me, is free to use his powers to the fullest extent to which he can develop them, and is capable of rational, moral decision-making. Furthermore, Fromm says that modern society has a definite lack of optimism about the capacities of man to be productive.

". . . the absence of visions projecting a 'better' man and a 'better' society has had the effect of paralyzing man's faith in himself and his future." (*Man for Himself,* page 90)

I take this as a personal challenge from Erich Fromm to me to find a vision of a better "myself" and a better society in the teachings of my Jewish heritage and my own personal experience. To be productive, however, I must put my powers to work. I must act, and this I intend to do.

Probably one of the most important factors which has recently reinforced my decision to declare myself as a Consciencious Objector is my marriage in September, 1969. I am no longer a single person, responsible only for myself or for all of mankind in a general way. I have the responsibility to build the best kind of world that I can for my wife and the children which we will someday have. This cannot be done through bloodshed, as I have tried to show. I do not want my children to live in such a world. I feel that war must be abolished, and that the only way to abolish it is to start right now by trusting and loving my fellow men. I cannot kill them, but must deal with them openly and honorably, and with a recognition of the intrinsic, infinite value of every human life.

Thus, I can unequivocally say that I am opposed to war in any form and can never condone or participate in it in any way.

"If You Would Like to Know"
By Chaim Nachman Bialik
(translated by the author of this C.O. statement)

If you would like to know the well
From which your slain brothers drew,
In the days of evil, strength such as this, and force of soul
To go out happily to meet death, to bare the neck
To every polished knife, to every outstretched ax,
To go up on the block, to jump into the bonfire,
And with "Echad"[1] to die the death of saints.

---

[1]Echad—The prayer "Hear O Israel, the Lord our God, the Lord is one," which martyrs have traditionally been said to have recited as they were killed.

If you would like to know the well
From which your suppressed brothers drew,
Between the straits of hell and the distress of slaughter,
  among scorpions,
The comforting of God, security, strength and greatness of
  spirit,
And the strength of iron to put out a hand to all toil, a
  shoulder
Stretched out to suffer a life of filth and revulsion, to suffer
Without end, without limit, without finish.

If you would desire to see the bosom to which were spilled
All of the tears of your people, its heart and soul, and its
  bitterness—
Where as flowing waters, its roars broke forth
Roars that tear the innards out of the depth of hell,
Groans that would frighten even the devil,
Rocks would be smashed, but not the hard heart of the
  enemy,
Stronger than rock, harder than the devil.

If you should like to know the fortress
Into which your fathers escaped carrying their souls,
Their Torah, their holy of holies—and were saved,
If you would desire to know the hiding place in which was
  saved—
And in the midst of its purity—the spirit of your mighty
  people,
Which also, in their having enough of a life of disgrace, spittle
  and insult,
Its old age did not give back the desires of its youth.

If you would desire to know the merciful mother,
The old mother, loving and faithful,
Who, with great mercies collected the tears of her lost son,
And with great loving-kindness prepares all his steps,
And with his ashamed return, worn out and tired,
Under the shadow of her roof she will ease his tears,
Cover him with the shadow of her wings, put him to sleep on
  her knees.

Hey, brother, we shall answer! If you do not know these—
To the Synagogue run, the old and ancient,
During the long nights of Tevet,[2] the desolate,
And in the burning days of Tamuz,[3] blaring down,
In the heat of the day, at dawn, or in the soul of the night,
And if God has still allowed a remnant to escape from
    sorrow—
Than perhaps also today your eyes will see within
In the abundance of the shadows of its walls, in the fog,
In one of the corners or next to its stove,
Lonely sheaves, like a shadow of what was lost,
Bowing Jews, faces shriveled and beleaguered;
Jews, children of the Dispersion, carrying the weight of its
    yoke,
Forgetting their toil in a withered page of G'morah[4]
Forgetting their poverty in the Midrash stories of old[5]
And whispering their worries in the prayers of Psalms.
(Ah, how cursed and lowly is this sight

In the eyes of the stranger—he won't understand!)
Then your heart will tell you
That your feet are walking on the threshold of the house of
    our life.
And your eyes will see the treasures of our souls.

And if God has not taken all the spirit of His holiness from
    you
And more still, from His comfortings in your heart,
And a spark of longing for the truth of days better than these
Will come still sometimes leveling its darkness.
Then know and hear, hah, my questioning brother,
That this is only a spark that has been saved;
        only a small sparkling remnant

---

[2]Tevet—A winter month on the Hebrew calendar.
[3]Tamuz—A summer month on the Hebrew calendar corresponding
roughly to the month of July and August.
[4]G'morah—part of the Talmud
[5]Midrash—A collection of stories with morals told by the ancient rabbis.

Which by a miracle escaped from the great fire
Which always illuminated your fathers on their altar.
And who knows if the rivers of their tears
Did not carry and bring us here today,
And in their prayer to God were we asked
And with their death were we commanded to life—
The eternal life!

Question #3

"To what extent does your religious training and belief restrict you from ministering to the sick and injured, either civilian or military, or from serving in the Armed Forces as a noncombatant without weapons?"

There is nothing in my religious training and belief that would restrict my ministering to the sick and injured as a civilian. In fact, this is of the highest consonance with my religious beliefs concerning the value of human life which I explained in answer to Question #1. But as I also said in my answer to that question, I can neither kill another human being, nor can I aid any other person or organization to do so. I, therefore, state emphatically that I cannot under any circumstances, or in any capacity serve as a member of, or under the orders of the Armed Forces.

While healing the sick and injured is commendable, to heal wounded or sick soldiers so that they can return to battle to kill or be killed would be a flagrant violation of my principles. I am willing, however, to serve as a civilian ministering to any and all persons who need my services, but not if they will go to battle that much sooner as a result of what I have done.

Furthermore, this position which I take applies also to any other task or situation as a noncombatant in the Armed Forces, because, by performing such tasks, I would be aiding the effort to kill human beings.

Question #4

"Have you ever given expression publicly or privately, written or oral, to the views herein expressed as the basis for your claim? Give examples."

I have never made any formal statements over my signature as to my beliefs and convictions on the issue of war and the killing of human beings other than in answer to the questions in this form.

I have, however, on many occasions discussed the issues both publicly and privately with my Hebrew school and Religious school students, friends, my wife, my parents, and my advisor, Rabbi Albert Axelrad. I have asked many of them to write directly to you verifying this fact.

I have on several occasions discussed the issue with my Hebrew and Religious school students in various congregations in the Boston area over the past two years. In every case I was careful to make my position explicit at the end of the discussion, so that the students could realize that this is what I truly believe, and that there are real live people who hold this belief.

In addition, I have counseled several of my friends to consider conscientious objection as a viable legal alternative to military service if their backgrounds and beliefs so warrant.

1. My feelings towards violence are essentially similar to a statement found in the writings of Erich Fromm, the Jewish religious-humanist author, "A pacifist standpoint . . . holds that force is either absolutely wrong, or that aside from cases of the most immediate self-defense its use never leads to a change for the better." I believe that there is an important difference between violence on the one hand, and force on the other. I feel that if force is necessary to prevent violence, then it is acceptable; if, for example, by blocking a punch I can avoid being hit, I would, but I would not strike back. If I could prevent a third person from being injured by an assailant, I would feel justified, if not compelled, to do anything in my power short of aggressive and senseless violence, to prevent the third person from being hurt. Defensive force is different from aggressive violence, in that it is solely a restraining measure, whose purpose is not to destroy or hurt another human being.

My feelings towards violence are a result of 13 years of

Jewish religious training, which I shall further describe in answer to question #2. In particular, several of Judaism's more important values as expressed in the Bible have had a profound impact on my life. The most basic of all is the Fifth Commandment, "Thou shalt not murder." My belief also derives from the Biblical prophet Isaiah, "It shall come to pass . . . that they shall beat their swords into plowshares, and their spears into pruning-hooks; nation shall not lift up sword against nation, neither shall they learn war anymore" (Isaiah 2:2, 4). (So important is this religious vision, that it is repeated by still another Biblical prophet, Micah.) I feel that the vision of Isaiah, combined with Psalm 34, verse 15: "Seek peace and pursue it" imply a specific injunction from God to mankind, that it is the responsibility of man to bring about a messianic age. There will be no Messiah who will arrive on earth and bring with him peace and love forever. It is up to man to bring about a messianic age through his own actions, one of the most basic of which is to seek peace, and not to participate in war. The Biblical quote most meaningful to me is almost a direct statement of this concept. It is Deuteronomy, Chapter 30, verses 15 and 19: "Behold I have set before thee this day life and good, and death and evil. . . . I call heaven and earth to witness against you this day, that I have set before thee life and death, the blessing and the curse; therefore choose life that thou mayest live." I refuse to participate in violence as an affirmation of life, as commanded by God in this Biblical passage.

In conjunction with my belief that man must act to bring about a messianic age, I also feel that all people are the children of God, and that no person has the right to deprive another of life.

In summation, I am an objector to war, unalterably, based on my Judaic upbringing, and opposed to any organization or training which teaches men to destroy life.

2. I have received Jewish training at Temple Israel in Boston since I was five years old, and the members of my entire family, (including not only my parents, sister, and brother, but also my

grandparents, uncles, aunts, and cousins) are observant in Reform Judaism. The Central Conference of American Rabbis (the Reform Jewish Rabbinical association) stated recently "Conscientious objection to military service is in accordance with the highest interpretation of Judaism."

I have also spent a total of five summers at Camp Tevya, a Jewish camp, where the moral and ethical teachings of Judaism were further taught to me.

In my last three years of high school I became active in the youth group of my temple, the Reform Youth Fellowship of Temple Israel, and in the New England Federation of Temple Youth, with which my temple group was affiliated. I found the experience of being in these groups particularly valuable in making Judaism alive for me, and in them I learned a great deal about ritual and ethical Judaism. I am presently attending Brandeis University, and chose to do so in part because of the Judaica courses available.

I have been a member of the Jewish Peace Fellowship for the last year and a half, and have spent a great deal of time in past years, especially last year, in organizing anti-war activities at my high school, The Roxbury Latin School.

I have been influenced a great deal by reading Joan Baez's autobiography, in which she describes her childhood, and how she became a pacifist. I found her message to be inspirational, and I hope that I can live up to the ideals expressed in that book.

3. I believe that the Armed Forces are an institution whose only goal can be death. Any participation in such an institution implies acceptance of those goals. I believe in accordance with Judaic tradition that if one sees evil and does nothing to stop it, one is as guilty as the evildoer, which would absolutely prohibit any participation in the military in any capacity.

I do not mean to say that I would not help a wounded soldier. My conscientious objection to war is an affirmation of the rights of all men to life. I only feel that I could do so solely in a civilian capacity.

Selection VI

4. Religious Training and Belief

a. Describe the nature of the belief that is the basis of your claim.

The basis for my claim as a conscientious objector concerns the broad question of whether my participation in the Armed Forces is consistent with my own beliefs based upon religious training, educational background, and upbringing. I have been struggling with this problem since the prospect of military service became imminent. It is now evident that my beliefs as a Jew and a physician make it impossible for me to participate in war in any form.

In order to make the nature of my claim clear, I must first explain how certain feelings, non-religious in essence, and circumstances led me to accept a commission in the Air Force. At the time of my first association with the Air Force, in the fall of 1968, I had just made application to and been refused admission to the Public Health Service, Division of Indian Health. Having decided that I was not going into Obstetrics and Gynecology, my Berry Plan deferment terminated. Those were the circumstances.

Now, I am compelled to explain how a very deep relationship with my family, which incidentally is founded in traditional Jewish teaching and philosophy, led me to accept a commission in the Air Force. Only then can one clearly see how further transcendent beliefs founded in Judaism led me to the complete rejection of support of violence and war.

151

As will become obvious later in connection with the origins of my beliefs in non-violence, my parents have always been a major consideration in my life. However, since my brother, and only sibling, passed away suddenly our ties became even stronger, and on my part there was a great need to please them. Compounding this, there is the cultural aspirations of one generation to pass their values along to the next. Based on these and other motivating factors, of which I may never be aware I made a decision. All other feelings were rationalized by saying that I could escape as a physician with little emphasis based on being a soldier. It was from this point spiritually that I embarked upon my military duty, a decision based upon extreme dependency. Only now after several months of participation and soul-searching can I look back with objectivity and see that certain irrevocable beliefs based on Jewish teaching cannot be repressed. These beliefs, now placed in the proper context, are the basis of my claim.

There are four basic tenets of the Jewish religion which form the framework of my claim. These are best summarized in the book *Two Paths to One God* by Rabbi Raphael N. Levine. First, Man should obey the moral law expressed in the Ten Commandments and Golden Rule, following the moral and ethical disciplines which they espouse. Second, one must invest life with such dignity, beauty, and goodness that it will be sanctified and reflect the holiness of God. Third, one should strive to attain God-like qualities in so far as it is possible for man to do. Fourth, man must help to fulfill the age old hope for justice and freedom, peace and human brotherhood. In Temple, these ideals are exemplified in the traditional orthodox sense respectively: to do the will of God, to hallow His name, to imitate Him, and to advocate God's kingdom on earth. As Rabbi Levine further states: "Worship is not confined to the temple or synagogue. It may be practiced in the privacy of the home, in the solitude of meditation, in the workshop or the garden. Every reverent thought is a prayer; every impulse to goodness is an act of worship."

The Ten Commandments which are embodied in the Mosaic

Code give us a framework from which to build a moral foundation. I could not express my application of the Commandments in relation to war and violence better than has been stated by Rabbi Stephen Wise, then president of the American Jewish Congress: "We of the Jewish brotherhood know that every command of our faith runs counter to war, that war is the supreme repudiation and negation of religion, forasmuch as war commands man to kill, to hate, to lie, to covet, to steal, and that until war goes, the prophecy and faith of our fathers cannot be fulfilled; 'and no man shall slay his brother.' " The first expression of the Golden Rule is documented in Rabbinical works prior to the time of Jesus, and is the cornerstone of the Judeo-Christian tradition. As a physician these teachings have special meaning. The Oath of Hippocrates tells us to "use treatment to help the sick according to my ability and judgment, but never with a view to injury and wrongdoing." One need only look to the Golden Rule and this is a natural progression. It is my firm belief that I must do nothing to contribute to the net increase in disease, disability or untimely death of human beings. As a military physician I save lives in order to destroy lives, in the strictest sense. In the most liberal sense, I am forced, in contradiction to my religious and ethical code to give aid and support to a net increase in disease, disability and untimely death.

To invest life with dignity, beauty and goodness and in so doing strive to attain as godly qualities as humanly possible, provides the framework upon which to build a life style. Each Jew, our religion teaches, adds to the sum of human goodness by helping to make the world a little better because he has lived in it. In this vein, Dr. Jerome Frank, Professor of Psychiatry at Johns Hopkins School of Medicine, states: "The essence of the non-violent approach to the resolution of conflict is to meet violence with calm courage and willingness to accept suffering, without ceasing to resist, but also without hating the attacker. By demonstrating to his adversary that he is willing to suffer for his beliefs, and that he is concerned for his attacker's welfare as well as his own, the practitioner of non-violence tries to weaken the will of his persecutor and to win him over, not to beat him down." This philosophy I have found to be a great value in my dealings as a physician and citizen of the world community. Out of it comes my beliefs in the worth of man and faith in his ability to solve complicated problems in a non-violent atmosphere. Ultimately, it is the hope for fulfillment of justice, and freedom, peace, and human brotherhood.

The Union Prayer Book is a cornerstone of modern Judaism. In one of the Friday night services contained in it Jews are urged to heed the words of prophets and seers, Jewish or of another religion. Traditionally, we are taught that prophets were men consumed with a passion for righteousness and overwhelmed by a compulsion to proclaim truth regardless of the consequences to themselves. They were not philosophers or theologians, but men whose depth of religious conviction and experience compelled them to speak out.

In my own life the teachings of contemporary prophets have had a great influence on my belief in non-violence and opposition to war in any form. Their lives and teachings have been a very real and vivid part of my life. The life of Gandhi is well known. His devotion to a life of non-violence and the huge strides he and his people made through its use are ultimately involved in my beliefs. Albert Schweitzer, a contemporary Jewish prophet in the truest sense, warns us about the mistrust among men that leads to war. He beseeches man to find a new spirit in dealing with his brother, "to rediscover the fact that we—all together—are human beings, and we must strive to concede to each other what moral capacity we have."

The life and deeds of Martin Luther King, Jr., a contemporary religious prophet, are outstanding. He stated that the choice is between "non-violence and non-existence." I have made my choice. It has been difficult to explain my beliefs, but I am sincere.

b. Explain how, when, and from whom or from what source you received the training and acquired the belief that is the basis of your claim.

The basic values and teachings that make up my belief have come from my religious training, family background and education. However, it was not until recently, during the period that I have been in the Air Force, that I have become unalterably opposed to violence and war of all types.

My religious training was at Temple Adath Israel. Under the guidance of Rabbi Joseph Rauch, and after his death, Rabbi Herbert Waller, I learned of Jewish history and tradition, Hebrew, the language of the ancient Jews, Jewish holidays and festivals, and about the relationship of Jews to the world and to other religions. The most meaningful of my years in Sunday school was the tenth grade, taught by Dr. Waller in preparation for Confirmation. We traced the history of the Jews in their struggles of the past. In our study of the holidays and festivals, Passover was outstanding as a time to pray for peace. Dr. Waller, as an active and vibrant part of the community, brought to our attention the relationship of contemporary problems with the past. Each member of the class was a participant in the worship service to celebrate our Confirmation.

From my family's example I have been able to transfer these essentially religious teachings into a workable life style. From my family I have learned the importance of strong meaningful relationships and the value of human life above all else. My father is a physician and honestly one of the most humanitarian individuals I have ever had personal contact with. Although, we are not in agreement in the implementation of my present beliefs, I feel extremely fortunate as his son. His own contemporaries have recognized him as President of the Jefferson County Medical Society and Vice President of the Kentucky Medical Society. On Sunday afternoons I would go with him to the hospital. Here I began to learn about total devotion to the needs of others, his ideal, and now one of mine. One of the most vivid memories of my childhood was a trip that the family took to Berea, Kentucky one summer where my father was giving free health care to the indigent people of the area. Not only has my father imparted to me this ideal of giving freely of one's self to the needs of others, but also he has taught me to be firm in my convictions no matter how unpopular they may be.

In a most traumatic way, that being the untimely death of my brother at the age of eighteen, I have learned the value of human life. That this event had a huge impact upon me is obvious. It led to several years of loneliness and searching, but ultimately to an understanding of the importance of life and the relation of one life to another. Through introspection into my own loss of a loved one I have come to know and understand that everyone is important. Whenever a person dies, their loved ones suffer the same loss that I have. This is true no matter how remote their existence may be. The death of my brother greatly altered my relationship with my parents. A sort of interdependence developed. And as I have mentioned earlier this is the basis for my decision, in spite of all other feelings to enter the Air Force.

As a child my summers were spent at Camp Nebagamon in Wisconsin. There, owner-director Max Lorber, pours his philosophies into every endeavor. Following his retirement he became a director of the Office of Economic Opportunity. At camp emphasis was on non-competition, thus avoiding the anxiety provoking situation of daily conflict. Campers were taught respect of individuality and the rights of others. There was a scholarship fund which afforded boys less fortunate than ourselves the opportunity of camping. Following my senior year in high school I was a counselor there and was afforded the opportunity of implementing the camp ideals.

Finally, through participation in the Air Force I have come to realize that I can not participate in war in any form. Upon arrival at Brooks Air Force Base in San Antonio I was given two weeks of instruction in duties and responsibilities of an Air Force officer. I quote from the indoctrination manual for officers of the USAF Medical Service: "The Communist world appears to be stronger today than it has ever been. Thus, it becomes your personal task to help fight the cold war and prepare yourself *to fight a hot war if it comes*. There is nothing easy or nice about this struggle. The cost is high and is paid for in both money and blood. Many people have already paid the supreme price." This literally as well as ideologically removes the physician from the role of non-combatant. Further, in nothing more than daily functions as a medical officer I have come to view my role in the military clearly. Whether in a war zone or a stateside assignment the function of the medical corps, as stated in the Army Field Manual "is a supporting service of the combat elements . . . concerned with mainte-nance of the health and fighting efficiency of the troops, to conserve manpower for early return to duty, to contribute *directly to the military effort* by providing adequate medical treatment and rapid orderly evacuation for the sick and wounded." In the Air Force I have seen at daily briefings, this same philsophy holds true. Again and again we are instructed that no matter how big or small the jobs or in what capacity, it is in direct support of the primary mission—flying, and ulti-mately the destruction of human life. All of this places me in a position which contradicts my religious training and beliefs. In all good conscience I cannot continue to support this effort.

d. Under what circumstances, if any, do you believe in the use of force?

The use of force is a difficult concept to deal with on a theoretical basis. In many situations its use has positive effect. All of the men whose principles I follow are very forceful. However, in the context of this question I assume it refers to physical force. As I have tried to explain I believe very funda-mentally in man's capacity to reason through interpersonal conflicts rationally. Of course, basic aggressive drives exist in all of us. On the level of personal defense, or the defense of a loved one, from physical attack this aggressiveness would probably supersede rational behavior. War cannot be equated with this type of behavior. It is either mass organized aggres-sion or retaliation; something which requires learning. Certainly if we can condition rats to repress their aggressive drives, we as mature, rational humans can sublimate our own aggressions.

e. Describe the actions and behavior in your life that in your opinion most conspicuously demonstrates the consistency and depth of your religious convictions that gave rise to your claim.

Behavior is a result of one's credo, both of which come from learning processes. Inasmuch as I hope my learning process will always continue, then my behavior will be constantly modified. Early behavior reflects learning in its rudimentary state whereas the behavior of an adult stems from much deeper consideration. My early behavior which stemmed from religious training was very structured. It involved participation in Sunday School worship and celebrational services, as well as didactic classes during the year prior to confirmation. I took part in a Jewish social club which placed emphasis on community philanthropic service. With maturity this behavior based on early religious teaching has found new avenues of expression. I have attempted to incorporate the beliefs into all of my actions. In answering the previous questions I have tried to relate the behavior which resulted from religious teachings and beliefs.

Of major importance in my life have been the influences of my family background and my decision to pursue a medical career. Because I have always planned to become a physician, my major areas of study have been concerned with my relationship to the world and to service of mankind. During one summer while in medical school I worked at the Kentucky State Hospital for the Mentally Ill, a service which very few physicians desire to render. Because these people receive such inadequate attention, this experience reinforced my belief in the importance of trying to help all people no matter how hopeless their illness may seem. As a junior and senior student and then intern I was able to practice medicine according to the views that I hold. In Detroit, as an intern I performed physical examinations on ghetto children so that they would be able to participate in an experimental Head Start Program. A final example of the expression of my belief came quite coincidentally. This past November, while waiting for a plane in Houston, Texas, a fellow traveler suddenly slumped to the ground, apparently dead. I and a colleague, disregarding the possibility of future legal consequences, rushed to his aid and administered cardio-pulmonary resuscitation until an ambulance arrived.

Lastly, and probably the most significant action I have ever made in support of my beliefs is the submission of this application for discharge on the basis of conscientious objection. I realize fully that I must accept any consequences that come as a result of this action and only through much thought and extreme dedication do I act upon my beliefs. Previous behavior and actions have been evidence for my beliefs. I now stand on them and in making this application give proof to my beliefs.

f. Have you ever given public expression, written or oral, to the views you have expressed herein as the basis of your claim? If so, specify when and where.

Prior to entry in the Air Force most of my beliefs were expressed at the level of individual interrelationships, in my ordinary dealings with others as a citizen and as a physician. These have been elucidated in answering the previous questions. In addition, since the inception of the Viet Nam war I have publicly expressed my feelings by displaying the peace sign and bumper stickers asking for peace on my car. As a medical student I worked for Senator Eugene McCarthy, an ardent peace candidate, in his Indiana primary campaign in the spring of 1968. I openly canvassed neighborhoods talking to people, trying to arouse the national conscience toward a greater effort for peace, brotherhood, and human decency.

Once on active duty, I suppose because of guilt feelings and the final awareness of what my course of action must be in order to be true to my beliefs, I let my beliefs become more public. I have attempted to take a course of action publicly that is most consistent with my beliefs. The final expression is this open claim to my beliefs as a conscientious objector.

In San Antonio this past fall I participated in the effort of the United Farm Workers to be recognized by the California grape growers and farm management elsewhere including southern Texas. I was very fortunate to be able to attend a rally at which Cesar Chavez, leader of the United Farm Workers spoke. He is an outspoken advocate of non-violence in the same sense and magnitude as Gandhi and Martin Luther King, Jr. His presence and words were inspiring, how so mild and soft spoken a man could rally such masses of people who had until recent years accepted their oppression. Needless to say, this experience fortified my growing feelings of implementing my beliefs.

Finally, at a dining out given for the class at the School of Aerospace Medicine I gave further public expression to my beliefs. Looking around I was impressed by the thousands of dollars that had been spent for dress uniforms by physicians, the majority of whom would be in the Air Force for only two years. My thoughts then jumped to Biafra, South Carolina, and to the west side of San Antonio, where people are starving. During the after dinner toasts I was compelled to propose one. It was a prayer for peace in the world.

Selection VII

Addendum and Update to File of Saul Rubinstein*

Over the past year experiences and readings have further strengthened my beliefs that being a Conscientious Objector is the only correct way to act. I have met people who have been brutalized by war. They talk about killing as if it was a game. I met some victims of war at hospitals. No legs, no arms, and psychological damage have been done to these people. This further convinced me of the immoral acts of warfare and violence.

I have become more involved in the Jewish Peace Fellowship. I am being considered for the position of New York Coordinator of the Jewish Peace Fellowship. A letter from the Executive Director of the Jewish Peace Fellowship is included in this addendum. Also through meeting and making friends with other Jewish Conscientious Objectors, my beliefs have been reinforced. Some of my friends are Israelis who are Conscientious Objectors. We have discussed our beliefs for long hours. During the year I was involved with other members of the Jewish Peace Fellowship at a demonstration at the Cincinnati Federal Building. We prayed and a rabbinical student blew the ram's horn. We demonstrated and spoke out against all violence around the world.

In Los Angeles I am now in a joint master's program in Jewish Communal Service and Social Work. I picked this field

---

*It is wise and potentially helpful to keep Selective Service updated on your progress and maturation as a C.O.

ASA

so I could do something for people. I also chose this area to further my understanding of different types of people. It is important to learn how to get along and deal with people in a moral way.

During the Summer I was in the Jewish School of Communal Service in Los Angeles. During this time I did further study in Judaism. I also met many interesting people. One person whose writing influenced me is Rabbi Tamaret. He was a great Talmudic and Rabbinical authority. He lived until the 1930's. He wrote that it is wrong to serve in the military. He wrote that leaders of countries in the past got people to serve in the military by saying it was for G-d. He pointed out that taking human lives can never be good for humanity. This has further crystallized my beliefs.

In the rabbinic source *Tosefta*, Conscientious Objection is discussed. Jewish Law here states that one who holds a higher law is to be respected and encouraged. In *Tosefta* it states that even the most physically fit and courageous, if he be a *rachman*, a compassionate and gentle person, he should be exempted from military service. It states that exemption must be granted to those who refuse to engage in military duty because they cannot reconcile killing, even in war, with the ethics of their conscience. Those whose consciences did not allow them to kill others are free from military duty, as stated in *Tosefta*.

The Beth Din (Rabbinical Court) in Boston ruled on Conscientious Objection and Judaism in 1972. They ruled that not only is Conscientious Objection recognized in Judaism, but it is also encouraged in many instances. I am including an article from *Newsweek* about the Beth Din. The part on Conscientious Objection is underlined.

During the past year I worked at the Hillel House at the University of Cincinnati. I have come to understand the passions and needs of different people. Humanity is too wonderful to destroy. I counseled and talked to people with different personal problems.

Many things have happended in my family over the past year. My sister, Judy, married a Russian Jew, Gavriel. Judy was ordered out of Russia shortly after her marriage. Gavriel is under sentence for refusing to serve in the Soviet military. I have an uncle in New York, a rabbi, who trains rabbis. I came across some of his writings on why he believes serving in the military is against Jewish Law. He stresses that through religious beliefs and compassion one can solve problems better than by war and military might. I have also become more religious over the past year. I have tried to follow the Jewish precept that all that I do must be mindful of respect for all creations of G-d. This past year has confirmed my beliefs. My parents have always shown me the importance of mutual respect and peaceful actions when dealing with others.

Over the past few months I have had to demonstrate the strengths of my beliefs. I was offered the classification of 1H by the Selective Service System if I would drop my Conscientious Objector claim. I could not accept. I believe that to give up my beliefs on Conscientious Objection is like not admitting that I am a Jew. In Jewish Law it is a sin to give up your beliefs, even if you are threatened with death.

I am willing to do alternative service to further the health, benefit, and well-being of people. Humanity is too important to destroy.

Selection VIII

1. The decision to request release from military service was not easy. I have every reason to believe the Air Force will treat me well, personally and professionally. As a psychiatrist, however, I'm often called upon to pinpoint problems of conscience; in my case the diagnosis is clear. I find myself unable to participate in a system in which violence to others is the end product. By virtue of both my religious and professional training, I hold the sanctity of human life primary, whether the conflict is between individuals or nations. As such I am conscientiously opposed to war and violence in any form. My plea is for an alternative method of serving my country.

I consider the thoughts which have led to this request to stem from my early religious training, as a member of Orthodox Judaism, and more recently from my experience as a physician and psychiatrist.

As a youth I was required to study the Torah (Holy Scriptures) and the Talmud, the compilation of Jewish civil and religious law. The roots of nonviolent thought are abundantly clear in both. The Torah rejects not only homicide but also striking another person (Deuteronomy 25:3); it also explains why, "Whoever sheds man's blood, by man his blood shall be shed; for in the image of God made He man." (Genesis 9:6) Through the centuries Jewish interpretation of the Torah has been the subject of fierce debate, particularly in periods when there seem to be many transgressions. The Talmud embodies the kernel of these teachings as they have evolved to this moment in time. The lesson of nonviolence is reflected there in the story of Rabba, before whom a man appeared and said,

> "The governor of my city has told me to go and slay that person, or he will kill me." Rabba replies "Let them kill you but you must not kill others; for who tells you that your blood is redder than his, perhaps his blood is redder than yours." (Pessachim 25a, Sanhedrin 74a)

It is this belief in the sanctity of human life that guides my action, a belief reinforced by my experience as a physician and as a human being. To make a differentiation in my treatment of human beings, whether on racial or political grounds, is repugnant to both my religious and medical training. As the Wisdom of Solomon relates;

> Thou lovest all things that are,
> And abhorrest none of the things which thou didst make;
> For never wouldst thou have formed anything if thou didst hate it.

In the scientific world there has never been a single shred of lasting evidence to differentiate one group of human beings as more righteous, or deserving of life than another. Consequently, how can I participate in a system in which those designated "enemy" are righteously eliminated? No degree of personal or national enmity justifies the taking of a life; in fact it is the preserving of life that takes precedence over all other activity. Indeed, in the view of Orthodox Judaism it is a sin to kill, even under order or duress. Without doubt, unquestioned obedience and proper performance of one's duties is at the heart of military success. As a physician the likelihood of finding myself ordered to hurt another human being is remote. I feel, however, that active participation in such a system, where this is an important means to the hoped-for end (military success) is as undesirable as killing someone directly.

The Hippocratic Oath, to which I swore, cautions against evil done intentionally or spawned by self-interest. It is clearly in my self-interest to comply with a military commitment. As one who has done primary research in drug abuse, military affiliation presents a boundless opportunity for further investigation, professional achievement and prestige. Though no official orders have been received, I have notification that I would be stationed in a safe and fertile environment for such endeavors. However, my religious training and conviction as well as the physician's oath, forbid me to profit from a situation perpetuated by war; nor may I give tacit approval to human violence by participation in the rituals necessary to sustain it. My desire to function as a physician is undiminished but I ask for an alternative setting where I can honor my conscience while fulfilling my obligation to our country.

2. I am the oldest son of a practicing Jewish family. The first five years of my life, and considerable stretches after that were spent in the home of my maternal grandparents, both of whom were immigrants and Orthodox Jews. The household was bilingual, Yiddish (a mixture of German and Hebrew) and English being the two languages spoken. Life was conducted in accord with Orthodox Jewish law, the Sabbath was observed, as were the dietary restrictions. My great uncle, a rabbi, now deceased, was alert for transgressions in religious ritual or belief.

Formal religious training was begun at age 9 with my enrollment in the Hebrew School affiliated with the local Orthodox synagogue. Classes were two hours a day, five days a week. Saturday services were mandatory. Like many other 9 year olds I would rather have played baseball. I must admit, however, that in retrospect I learned something; I learned what it was like to be a Jew. The Hebrew School, situated in an ethnically mixed neighborhood, was intermittently besieged by adolescent attackers. The ritual was invariably the same, demands to kiss their religious symbols or spit on mine, followed by my "undiplomatic" refusal and the inevitable beating. Perhaps I could have avoided all that but I could do no more than protect myself from injury. I was forbidden to retaliate. Indeed, at the time, the consequences, according to the Talmud, seemed more frightening than physical harm.

That one has difficulty unlearning these beliefs was brought home to me at age 20 when I encountered a similar experience with similar results.

The above was not without its rewards, however. At 13, I became a bar mitzvah, ordained a man, in an Orthodox service. I had learned to speak and write Hebrew proficiently and had assimilated the moral, ethical and religious teachings which now appear to me to have led inevitably to my present objection. I attended a public high school but, unlike many of my peers, I remained active in the synagogue for a year after bar mitzvah. At fourteen, the grandparents that raised me both died of cancer and two events followed. I stopped going to synagogue and decided to become a doctor. For the next six years I remained angry at everything and everyone: the religion that had "let them down," the doctors who failed to save them and myself because I felt helpless.

I was the first member of my family to attend college; I had a scholarship and worked for a good part of the rest. While majoring in biology, I also found time for a good deal of anthropology. Both areas have no tolerance for superstition, prejudice and the concept of inherent good or evil. I was very much impressed with the writings of Konrad Lorenz and to this day quote his work to my classes at Boston University's Metropolitan College.

Lorenz called attention to the fact that only two animals have demonstrated that they destroy members of their own species, the European Brown Rat and Man. Since this event is so rare in nature he postulates the existence of a "Species Protective Mechanism." Under most circumstances this mechanism remains intact in human beings, but under certain conditions it begins to break down and we become capable of destroying our fellow man. The steps involved are as follows;

a) a group of human beings find themselves in a prolonged unresolved conflict
b) they begin to identify themselves as different from another human group

c) there is increasing polarization and during this process we begin to see;

d) the labeling of the other group as something less than human, (this dehumanization will later make it easier to kill)

e) there is a crisis event which triggers the release of the Species Protective Mechanism and allows for the condition in which men are willing to kill each other in open warfare.

It is just this form of dehumanization that my religious teaching warns against. It is Gad, one of the twelve sons of Jacob who warns, "If a man sin against thee, cast forth the poison of hate and speak peaceably to him, and in thy soul hold no guile." (Testament of Gad 6:3). Consequently, for me to become actively involved in a military endeavor, where men are attempting to resolve their conflict by shedding each other's blood, is to admit defeat and renounce the principles I have tried to live by.

In addition to my personal life I find myself dealing with these issues in the practice of psychotherapy. The patients are invariably in conflict. Part of my task is to help them recognize that it can be peaceably resolved. For many this has been a lifelong struggle and they have identified themselves as alien from the rest of society; my job is to demonstrate that they still have a place in humanity. Frequently, patients have defined themselves (or everyone else) as "sick" or different; my job is to remove the supports from these labels. Occasionally this dehumanization of themselves or others sets up a situation in which additional stress will lead to suicidal or homicidal behavior. Seeing that this does not happen encompasses my responsibility both as a physician and as a human being. One can readily see therefore, that in many respects my concept of therapeutic work is antithetical to a military posture, where violent solutions to conflict are often sought.

In the course of psychiatric training one is faced with a steady stream of moral and ethical dilemmas. Confidentiality, the patient's welfare as opposed to society's and the issue of involuntary hospitalization are included among these. Confronting these problems often causes one to examine his own belief and action. As in the patient, eventually these crystallize and one must give up rationalization and compromise as a way of behaving. For me, my experience as consultant to a local district court has been a turning point. In frequent contact with the criminally accused, often violent men, I have listened to their accounts of destructive behavior toward others and their subsequent self-destroying guilt. They have, on their own, passed through Lorenz's five stages and the result has been, not resolved conflict but profound inner torment. This torment is then expressed verbally and in their self-defeating behavior. As a consultant for the Massachusetts Rehabilitation Commission I also see them after they have passed through the prison system, a trifle more crafty but no less alienated or hostile. This experience has further corroborated my earlier religious conviction and training that violence, whether individual or institutional, is demeaning to the nature of man and destructive to the human soul. Intense contact with this problem on an individual level, and the nightly news reports of the same conflicts throughout the world have only reinforced my conviction that the Scriptures were right in pointing out that;

> "He who returns evil for evil, evil will not depart from his house."
> "Neither is it good for the righteous to punish." (Proverbs 17:13 and 17:26)

After considerable thought I find that I cannot compromise these religious and ethical teachings which are at the heart of my belief. The experience of my early life and now within my profession suggests that there is a need for someone to declare "I am for life," "I trust in the inherent good of man," "I will take a chance that he will not do me harm." It is only in this way that life may be experienced at its highest level of human potential. For me, this can only be done by observation of the religious and ethical principles I live by.

In matters of conviction regarding my claim I have relied for religious guidance on Rabbi A. Axelrad, Chaplain of Brandeis University, Waltham, Massachusetts. He has been of invaluable help and support.

In considering my present position I asked myself whether the Scriptures and their prohibition against violence were meant to be applied in every situation. Is the legal and moral issue so clear (as WWII must have seemed to most, but not all Jews), what then? Again the training that I received in childhood enjoins;

> "it is not good for the righteous to punish, (and) it is evil for the righteous to be a vehicle of punishment (Psalms 5;5)

In my personal and professional life I have believed in the use of restraining force, when its intent is to prevent harm to myself or others. Under this doctrine I have, on occasion, sent people to psychiatric hospitals against their will, in accordance with the laws of the state, and the accepted responsibility of my profession for the good and protection of both the patient and society. I have done this, however, with considerable reservation as to the ethics involved, for who can divine where the rights of an individual should be compromised? Nevertheless, this sort of restraining force must be clearly differentiated from the punitive measures that might be taken by those who feel "right" and the retaliatory force of those who have been hurt or transgressed against. It is my unshakeable feeling that war in any form and as presently practiced, is inimicable to these concepts.

While I have never been a "joiner" or "activist" in the commonly accepted sense of the terms there is ample evidence that I have persevered in beliefs that I have held despite the personal consequences. My refusal to accept idolatry or to debase my religious beliefs can only be documented by the personal testimony of others. In college I participated in peaceful protest against racial discrimination practiced by local merchants. I did this at some risk in an environment that was basically hostile and belligerent. Again, in college, I ran for class president on the platform that it was a useless, de facto position, and that if elected, I would resign to demonstrate the need for meaningful student government. I was elected, kept my pledge and more responsibility was accorded my successor. In 1963, though threatened, I defended the right of a known communist to speak on the campus. I was not supporting his brand of dogma but his right to be heard.

More recently I have worked without recompense for a six month period in a free medical clinic because I believe that certain groups are discriminated against by our city's hospital system.

Though I have not aired my religious or ethical prinicples publicly, my views on violence, the causes of aggression, their interrelation with drug use and the breakdown of Lorenz's Species Protective Mechanism are known to the forty members of my "Drug Culture" course at Boston University. I hope to supply confirmatory evidence of all these points in subsequent letters of reference. I hope the board will consider these in reviewing my application for discharge with alternative service.

Selection IX

1. I am an Orthodox Jew. I am a descendant of a long Rabbinical line with a strong Jewish tradition. The nature of my belief includes the precept that I cannot take the life of another human being under any circumstances. I believe that if I were ordered to take part in any way in an action which may destroy a human life I should refuse, even if I may be hurt as a result.

It is my duty to love all of G-d's creations. I must empathize and understand my fellow men and women. In short, as Hillel, one of our great rabbis said: "The whole of Jewish teaching is: What is hateful to you do not do to others."

I attended religious school, the Chofetz Chaim Day School of Cincinnati, (now the Cincinnati Hebrew Day School) full time for ten years. Among the basic areas of study were the teachings on the importance of peace. Such statements as "Great is peace." Other commands of the Torah are conditional, but the peace command is unconditional. Seek peace and pursue it. (*Talmud Nezikim, Perek Hashalom.*) Another teaching in *Perek Hashalom* is "The world rests on three things; on justice, on truth, and on peace."

Another important influence on me has been the teaching that one is prohibited to shed another's blood. *Murder may not be practiced to save one's life.* A man came to Raba, a great Rabbi, and said to him, "The governor of my town has ordered me, 'Go and kill so-and-so, if not I will slay thee.' " Raba answered him: "Rather he kill you than you commit murder, who knows whether your blood is redder than his." (*Talmud Sanhedrin,* 74a.)

172

These two ideas of loving peace and refusal to shed another's blood are basic to my way of life.

2. One person who had a great influence on my beliefs was my grandfather, a prominent Orthodox rabbi. He was a leader of Orthodox Jewry in the United States and Canada until his death. My grandfather left me with the impression of the uselessness of violence. He taught me that it is against our Jewish tradition to take a human life, no matter what the reason or cause involved. He emphasized that only G-d had the power to take a life and no man may hold this power. My grandfather not only preached this but he showed this by example on different occasions. I was told both by my parents and my grandfather's followers of the time he was attacked by a woman on the streets of Cincinnati. She began hitting him with a crowbar. She broke some of his ribs and also an arm. The people who saw this said my grandfather had a cane and, as they put it, he could have struck her many times, but did not. He just tried to protect himself by covering his head with his hands. When he was asked why he did not strike her he said he could not take the chance of possibly killing her and also said that his violence would not have solved anything. My grandfather, using his own peaceful methods, was successful in saving lives and helping victimized people.

My parents are also Orthodox Jews. My father, who is a physician, always taught me that man's place on earth is to enable his fellow man to live better. Both of my parents have always counseled me that I must always use my mind, and never my physical stength, when dealing with fellow humans. I remember vividly how angry they would get if my brother and I would get into fights. They would pull us apart and make us talk out our problems and make up. They emphasized that I must act in this way toward all people. A few times I came home from school and told them I had a fist fight with someone. They emphasized how wrong this was and made me and the other person solve our disagreement by other means. They have taught me both by precept and example that I should always empathize with my fellow man. I have seen my parents become upset when even someone who had been unkind to them became ill or was hurt in some way. They tried to help this person. I have also seen them crying on occasions when they heard about the sufferings of someone almost anywhere in the world.

The ideal of helping my fellow man has led me to join such organizations as the Student Community Involvement Program. This program aims at alleviating the sufferings of people in need and helping them get along better with their family and neighbors. This year I started working with a young man at Longview State Hospital. One of the changes that I have noticed in him is that he is beginning to communicate with others on a verbal level. I am constantly telling him and demonstrating to him that there are better ways to communicate with others than by way of his fists. As I stated, he is beginning to try my way.

I attended an Orthodox Day School, Chofetz Chaim of Cincinnati, full-time from nursery school through the eighth grade. As I mentioned earlier, this is where I got most of my religious training. The religious school was founded and directed by my grandfather. A very important part of my school years was spent studying the Talmud, which is the collection of writings constituting the Jewish civil and religious law. During these years and ever since I have become influenced by many important Jewish figures mentioned in the Talmud. Rabbi Akiba was one of the most famous Rabbis mentioned there. He felt no man had the right to take a human life and even declared that if he had been in the Sanhedrin (Jewish Court) he would never have allowed anyone to be condemned to death. (*Mishna Makot*, 1:10). Another very great Rabbi was Hillel, who lived in the first century B.C.E. Tradition presents Hillel as the epitome of saintliness and scholarship. He often taught: "Be of the disciples of Aaron, loving peace and pursuing peace, loving thy fellow creatures." Hillel also taught that: "Do not unto your neighbor what you would not have him do unto you. This is the whole Law, the rest is commentary." Recently I have come to be influenced by articles I have read about the pacifist Rabbi Johanan ben Zakai. He lived at the same time as Rabbi Akiba. He accomplished much by preaching non-violence to the Jewish people in Israel when they were faced with Roman military might. By being non-violent he was able to continue to teach of the Law and also to set up a Jewish Center of learning in Israel. I would like to mention one more person in Jewish tradition, Gedaliah. He was governor of Judea after the destruction of the First Temple. The Bible describes him as a true pacifist. (*Jeremiah* Chapter 40 and 41, and *Kings II*, 35). He preached non-violence to the Jews when Babylonia took over. He was able to save the Jewish community in this way and keep it alive. To this day Orthodox Jews fast in memory of the assassination of this great man.

Not only studies but also experiences have helped me crystallize my position. Six years ago I was visiting at in Jewish Hospital, in Cincinnati, when I saw a group of policemen standing in one of the emergency treatment rooms. I inquired what happened and was informed that the police had "had to" shoot a wanted criminal. I saw the body. I became sick to my stomach and for months could not go into the Jewish Hospital. To this day I become very upset when I pass the emergency room. Even though this man was a known criminal, who society "didn't need," it still was very upsetting to me to see what had happened. I looked into myself and began to remember all that was taught to me. I knew there was a better way to handle people than by the taking of their lives. Now I had seen what death was. It was real and no longer something you see on television or in the movies.

In 1968, during the summer, I lived on a Kibbutz, a collective farm in Israel, which had 800 people on it. These people respected each other as individuals and solved their mutual problems by discussion and not by physical violence. Their society seemed to me ideal. A year later, in 1969, a friend of mine was killed by a sniper on the Suez Canal. His family could hardly take the shock. I wondered what he died for. There was no peace; in fact more fighting and death and destruction on both sides continued.

Not only in the Middle East but all over the world people kill each other uselessly. Two years ago someone I knew could not stand the killing any more. He felt special abhorrence of the massacres in Biafra. One morning he went to the Synagogue in New York and there resolved that he must make the world feel these horrors and stop them. That afternoon he did a shocking thing. Knowing that it was against Jewish Law, but also feeling he could not tolerate the inhumanity of man to man, he burned himself in front of the United Nations. This act, by my friend, has left an indelible scar on me.

3. My religious beliefs prevent me from being an accomplice to killing. I cannot be part of any group which may harm a human life. The Judaic teachings state that a bystander, who could prevent a killing and does not, is just as guilty as if he himself had shed the blood. All the more so if he helps people to get ready for battle. I cannot serve as a non-combatant in the Armed Forces since I believe that one is not allowed to have *any role* in an organization which uses excessive violence and takes human lives. (Talmud Sanhedrin 74a).

4. I have in many instances and places given my views on peace. In the past four years I have had to put my beliefs to the test. Twice I was bodily attacked, but refused to fight back. I just shielded myself with my hands and waited until my assailants stopped. I belong to organizations which preach peaceful behavior. One such group is the NAACP, which is constantly stating that only through peaceful means can constructive gains be made. I have spoken out against all wars and acts of violence. I have tried to help pure pacifist movements, such as the Jewish Peace Fellowship in any way possible. (The Jewish Peace Fellowship is a group founded in the 1940's which is dedicated to getting people and governments to see the need for a pacifist way of life). As I explained earlier, I belong to the Student Community Involvement Program at the University of Cincinnati. This organization is dedicated to the alleviation of the burdens of our fellow men and women.

Selection X

When War Comes*

Since my maiden speech before Rotary up in Ohio some six summers ago [1932], I've often debated with myself as to just what I'd like to discuss if the opportunity were ever offered me to speak before my own Rotary Club. More recently I've realized that I could present nothing with such appeal as those dancing girls Edley said he observed in Hawaii at such a distance. I wondered if I wouldn't like to take a word like "ability," put it on a chart in front of you and then, by standing on my head and using a megaphone, tell you what I think ability really means. It has occurred to me that I might comment on the remark made by President Mike in the Rotary News a few weeks ago when Edley was out of town. Do you recall reading about, "When the cat is away, the mice will play?" I'm sure you all noticed that Mike, referring to the cat, said something about canine tendencies, but we'll let that lapsus linguae go by unnoticed. I've often wanted to preach a sermonette on the text of "America," with which we open and close our meetings, with the purpose of once and for all impressing upon you the words of the last stanza. You know, the song starts out in the 1st person, "MY country tis of thee, sweet land of liberty, Of thee I sing," and while you're singing

---

*Selection X consists of some hitherto unpublished, but powerfully moving, writings on nonviolence, dating back to pre-World War II days, by Rabbi Stanley Brav. Now retired, Brav was for many years a distinguished Jewish peace proponent and activist.

177

it, the song performs an act of magic. It takes your mind off your own little personal self, makes you think of America, and by the last verse instead of being a rugged individualist you are a social creature, enarming your fellow citizens and joining with them, *OUR* fathers' God, To Thee, Author of Liberty, To Thee WE sing.

Well, I forego all these and other attractive subjects, to discuss something that is unpleasant, unpopular, ugly and, I hope, disturbing. You will agree with me, that the last presentation of the Committee on International Good Will, when Colonel Moses outlined the situation in Europe and in the Far East, was one of the most sane and lucid and illuminating talks in that field it has ever been our privilege to hear. If one were to draw a simple conclusion from his remarks, it would be this: War is being fought openly or through propaganda on many fronts of the world today, and unless we misinterpret the spirit of our times, we are headed for a second World War of calamitous proportions. When that will come, observers differ in predicting, but that it is coming they all agree. Peace machinery has broken down, dictators are on a rampage, treaties are regarded as scraps of paper, and every nation is arming to the teeth for what it calls its own protection. Today there seems to be only one force preventing the outbreak of a world conflict. Some of the nations are not quite prepared for it as yet. In a couple of years their naval, air and land forces will be in better shape. Then, anything can happen.

Now, if we accept this view of world affairs today—and trained observers are unanimous in accepting it—we can logically assume one of two attitudes. We can follow the mythical ostrich and bury our heads in the sand, saying, "Let it blow. Life is just a bowl of cherries. I can't be bothered with such matters." How did the old song go?—"driftwood on the sea of dreams." We are all driftwood, unable to stem the tides, moved by fate over which we have no control whatsoever. So let's forget the whole situation.

Some people come to this point of view because they are natural-born pollyannas, others because they want to borrow the horse's blinkers and see only what's in front of their noses, and nothing else, while with others it's a matter of moral and intellectual laziness. Let's call this whole attitude, the laissez faire attitude, just not bother our heads at all about these larger questions.

A second attitude, just as logical, is to say, Well, the world is in a mess. What can I *do* about it? Those of us who have taken this question seriously in the past have advocated all sorts of action. Help organize a decent League of Nations, and take the lead in keeping it decent. Join the World Court. Hold an economic conference to iron out the problems of populations, markets and raw materials that bother the have-not nations today. Set up an international police force to bring aggressors before the bar of justice. Keep America away from war, by neutrality. Give the people the last word in declaring war, via the referendum. Any of you who have been near the peace movement know that the kindly folks who have been working their heads off in peace-time in order to abolish war haven't gotten to first base with any of these proposals. When, as at the present time, they finally convince the country that profits should be taken out of war manufactures, a piece of legislation like the present May Bill is perpetrated on the nation. It pretends to take the profits out of war, but actually does not, while it sets up a war-time dictatorship over the people which may never return us the freedom of our democracy.

Well, why, you will ask, all the failure thus far to impress the majority of the people with these plans to turn our present international anarchy into a reign of international law and order? Let me cite you the reasons that come to my mind:

First, it's because we think that fighting is normal and natural and human and excusable when sufficiently provoked. A few weeks ago a fellow minister in this city whom I love and admire and respect said to me, "You know, I'm in favor of peace, but when I see what this fellow Hitler is doing my blood boils, and I don't know to what ends I wouldn't go to right the wrongs he's done." My friend was taking it for granted, at least in the back of his mind, that war is defensible when it is fought for a good and holy cause, forgetting that every nation tells its people it is fighting for a good and holy cause.

Another reason peace plans have failed is because millions still believe that the way to prevent war is to prepare for it. A billion dollars a year is Uncle Sam's current war bill, and the military and naval departments are always clamoring for more. And you know who else wants more: Bethlehem and United States Steel who build your battleships, the Duponts who make your explosives and Pratt-Whitney and others who make your bombing planes. But we can't single these out as culprits, because there is scarcely a man in this room today who does not believe in preparedness. We're all jumping on the bandwagon. We forget what Sir William Robertson, Chief of the British General Staff during the World War later confessed. "Instead of preventing war," he said, "we know that preparations are apt to precipitate it. Never in history were preparations so complete or so widespread as during the 50 or 60 years previous to 1914, and yet never were wars so frequent as in that period."

I'll give you yet a third reason why these peace plans have never captured the imagination of this country. It's because people who really want peace—and every one of you is in that number—haven't wanted it enough. You know the horror of war, especially you who have seen service. You know its cost in lives and property. You know the suffering it causes. You know that Sherman was right when he said, "War is hell." You know that war is murder and that murder is sin. But when the radios blast the news that war has come, when the bugles blow and the drums roll, you have told yourselves that you are going. You'll know all the excuses: it's the last resort; we're defending our wives and children; this time we'll really preserve democracy and fight to end all wars.

I level no charge at you personally that cannot be levelled at those who spend their entire lives for the cause of peace. These so-called peace-lovers are sincere enough and earnest enough, but are they honest enough? If they are honest, they'll admit that war is wrong, and there are no "ifs" and "buts." If they are honest, they will die rather than kill. If they are honest, they will not only refuse to fight under any circumstances, but they will refuse any non-combatant service whether at the front or behind lines, because it aids and abets an evil. If they are honest, they will let the government know where they stand now, so that the government will not count on them after war is declared. And if they are honest, they'll publish far and wide the fact that they repudiate that conception of patriotism which means the death and crippling of millions of their fellow citizens, and untold misery to tens of millions more.

Well, you say, it looks as if Stanley is an absolute pacifist, and if you are kindly disposed, you may wish me the courage to stand by my convictions in time of crisis. Frankly, I wish myself that courage, and wish it to every minister who is finished giving war the blessing of God. But I'll tell you this: knowing the vicious unpopularity of conscientious objection, those of us who take this position are doing everything in our power to prevent the crisis of war from ever occurring. Where will you be when war comes? I was much too young to be taken in 1917, but I was not too young to be influenced by the propaganda of that day. I've given each of you a copy of a magazine which illustrates how modern propaganda works. Let me leave you with the quotation of a song I've never forgotten—over 20 years—and which may be the challenge soon thrown at all of us. You once thrilled to these words. How will you feel when they are sung again?

> I know you love your land of liberty, I know you love your
>   U.S.A.
> But if you want the world to know it, now's the time to show it,
> Your Uncle Sammy needs you, one and all, answer to his call.
> It's your country and my country with millions of real fighting
>   men,
> It's your duty and my duty to speak with a sword not a pen.
> If Washington were living today, with sword in hand he'd
>   stand up and say,
> For your country and my country, I'd do it all over again.

Remarks delivered at a Rotary Club meeting in Cincinnati, Ohio, in 1938.

Religion and the European War

The solemn brooding seriousness with which millions in Europe look upon the present critical hour, has jumped with the speed of electricity to these shores. We are not in the same imminent danger of air-raids. Our own bodies are not immediately threatened. We do not face possible death this very night. Yet the pall of terror, caused by the beginning of military operations abroad, has struck our own hearts as if we were on the very scene of battle.

We have become so closely tied to Europe through the rapid improvement in communications that we have been able to follow the steps leading to the present outbreak with an almost minute-by-minute keeping abreast of the news. At this very second, our radios are pouring out the latest developments abroad with sharp, rapid-fire, staccato reports of recently received dispatches. In all probability, we are better acquainted with the actual situation in Poland, Germany, Italy, France and England than are the natives of those countries themselves. We can easily predict the shambles which Europe will soon find its principal cities to be, the unspeakable destruction of human life—both combatant and non-combatant, for pretty rules of honor will scarcely last 48 hours in a modern war; and we can readily envisage the overturn of all morality in Europe to the point where respect for human personality—the highest value among the moral teachings of all religions, respect for truth— the highest value among the teachings of all sciences, and respect for God and His unqualified Commandments, will be reduced to a level not only medieval but barbarian, as governments and populations give themselves over to the worship of Mars, the god of War.

The question we ask ourselves at this moment is whether we are humanly—physically or mentally—capable of being so self-composed as to submit to the exhortation of the prophet Isaiah, when, in an ancient critical hour, he said, "Come now and let us reason together." Is there yet time for us in America to subdue our emotions to the point of permitting our reasoning powers to function in our own behalf and in behalf of suffering humanity everywhere? Are we capable of the self-control that is required? Can we rise to the spiritual heights of this tense moment in human history? Are our souls of sufficient proportions to give us strength under the strain of these hours? Will we still be able to hear the still, small voice of God in our hearts, the voice of religion, when the roar of cannon and the crash of aerial bombs is already thundering in our ears?

I am not prepared to say, categorically, that America will consent to listen to the counsel of true religion in the difficult days ahead. If our so-called statesmen and diplomats bungle their trying tasks, as did Wilson and Page and House and the others back at the beginning of the World War, the likelihood is that we shall be asked to listen to the counsel of our stumbling, erring, blundering, power-drunk leadership, instead of heeding our consciences and the dictates of quiet reason. It is highly likely that British propaganda will once again sweep us off our feet. Even the most stolid and phlegmatic citizen among us is susceptible to the emotionalism of war. Perhaps it is just as well that we admit this inherent weakness of ours, at the very beginning. This morning, while walking to my study, I exchanged greetings with a fellow-townsman—a communicant of one of our largest churches—whom I had always judged to be of a most timid and retiring nature. He is a man well past fifty. "Well, it's started," he said to me, and his tones revealed how jittery his nerves were. "There's only one thing to do," he went on, and now there was vehemence in his voice as he said, "We've got to crush Germany." To this man, not only had the war started, but we Americans had already cast in our lot, and this gentle soul who would never have to fight as a soldier was already proclaiming his war-time patriotism.

My friends, this is a sign of rancor, the bitterness, the hatred that has seeped into the spirits of our fellow-countrymen—and into many of our own hearts—in the past few years. And it is these very emotions that will, when America stands on the brink of war, let us be passive if not actually enthusiastic in permitting our country to enter into horrors abroad. I would

defy any member of our community to exhibit a larger knowledge and understanding of the bestialities of the Hitler regime,
than it has been my situation as a teacher and Jewish leader to
have acquired, and yet I do not hesitate to say that hatred of
Germany, of the German people and even of the Nazi government leaders is as egregious a sin at this moment or will be at
any future hour, as it was when peace was still the hope of
Western Civilization. The only thing that decent men and
women dare hate is the vicious cruelty, the naked injustice, the
barbarous violence, the stark usurpation of human rights and
liberties that have existed in Germany, and it is the most
elemental lie of all war-thinking that you can destroy cruelty
with the unspeakable cruelty of war, destroy injustice with the
inevitable injustices of war, restore liberty by destroying liberties as becomes imperative in war, or crush violence with the
weapons of violent war. Sin begets sin. We will never create a
peaceful world by forcing people to swallow a bitter pill of
peace-after-defeat at the point of the bayonet. What is happening today in Europe will, whatever the outcome, only disrupt
the morals of the world, not for our time alone, but for the
entire lifetime of our children and our children's children.

I confess tonight that, knowing the history of Europe since
the days of the Caesars, knowing the story of modern nations
since the days of Napoleon, and knowing the temper of the
peoples abroad since the signing of the Versailles Treaty, I have
been unable, during the last nine years in which I have made a
constant study of conditions in Europe, to see any other
outcome than that which faces the world today. For fully seven
of those nine years, since I have been personally connected
with the peace movements in this country, I have been convinced that the only real issue in which some hope remained
for this country is not, "Will there be a war in Europe?"—
which is now answered for us, but, "Will America stay out?"—
which is partly within our own determination. You know as
well as I, the pressure that has already been exerted upon us by
the England which sent us its King to look at a few short weeks
ago, and you know how this pressure into war is bound to be

intensified. I have never held a brief for the position of the absolute isolationist who says that what goes on in Europe is none of our concern. This is the attitude of the proverbial ostrich burying its head in the sand. Even we Jews have learned that a rabbi or a Jewish street peddler cannot be abused in the streets of Berlin or Jerusalem or Algiers or Warsaw without our feeling the smart and sting, as remote as we are. In like manner, all America has learned that a war such as the present one cannot be fought in Europe without drastic reverberations in this country—even if we stay out completely. The world is too small today to permit one to live alone. When our neighbors are exchanging rifle shots, we may expect some of the shells to strike us, even if we are innocent bystanders.

On the other hand, we must be fully aware that we have made no military alliances with any European nation, even though England and France take it for granted America will never fight on the side of Germany. It cannot be doubted in the least that we are more friendly with our former allies now than we were in 1914—even in 1916—and that we feel more irked by the German government today than ever before, with the possible exception of the height of the submarine campaign in early 1917. But we must fully and firmly realize that there is nothing whatsoever inevitable about this country's joining in the slaughter that is now doomed. America, at this hour, is the one spot on earth where liberty and freedom are more than catchwords. If the threatened "M-Day"—mobilization day—should ever come to this blessed land, the first thing that would happen would be the destruction of this very liberty and this very freedom, with the very serious risk that it may take generations before they are returned to these shores. We, at that moment of mobilization, would be subscribing to the doctrines that force can only be combatted by force, and that peace can be created through violence—both of which are refuted by history and by reason, and are denied by religion. We shall—if that fateful day comes—be consenting to change the commandment from "Thou shalt not murder" into "Thou shalt murder." We shall—each of us, even those remaining over here—have our hands dripping with blood, even more bloody than they are today because of our failure to prevent the present situation. We shall be guilty of sin against God and against man that will be beyond expiation or atonement. All of this will be our shame and our immortal disgrace if we ever consent to pile American bodies upon the pyramid of those slain in the Second European War. Our only way to preserve the blessings of this land is to maintain the strictest, severest absolute neutrality—at almost any cost. The only accomplishment of joining a European War, no matter how the respective armies may be standing, will be to pour fuel upon a devastating bonfire by which, at these early hours, we are already singed.

We are already tainted with responsibility for this outbreak because America with large profits to gain has not made sufficient efforts to prevent hostilities, and because, in our weakness, we permitted the circumstances to arise whereby the present government in Germany could have come into power in the first place. This is evil enough in us, guilt enough. We dare not add to the blood that is already dripping from our hands.

America and Americans may not listen to the voice of true religion, and indeed, false prophets may again arise to ask God's blessing for the armies whose cause this nation may espouse. But true religion will stand its ground. "Not by power, nor yet by strength but by My spirit, saith God," will man learn to prevail. "Thou shalt not murder." "Thou shalt love thy neighbor as thyself." "Thou shalt be holy for I, the Lord, thy God, am holy." He who taketh the sword shall perish by the sword." "Have we not all one Father, hath not one God created us all?" This is the only position that a God-fearing man or woman can hold, and still remain true to God. There are no compromises with the large principles of religion. Men may put us to death, but if our convictions are rooted in God, they can never force us to kill, or to aid or abet the murder of war.

My friends, do not expect to hear from me any words regarding war and peace which differ in a single iota from this stand. Religion has disgraced its calling too frequently in the past with the hypocrisy of pretending God's sanction for whatever cause the nation may be espousing. The time for patriotism is not when the bugle blows, but now before the flag is unfurled. We must never relax our energies until we have carried America beyond the temptation of casting herself into the flames, when she can stand before the ruins and shambles of Europe with her hands the cleanest of all, with her example of liberty and freedom unbesmirched and undefiled, with her vision of the godly way of justice and love and cooperation and brotherhood undimmed, with her strength unimpaired to build again toward the Kingdom of Heaven on Earth.

Grant us peace, O Thou Eternal Source of Peace. Yea, grant Peace to the world, but grant us the courage and the strength to achieve Thy peace, in Thy way. Amen.

Living on the Brink of War

As central in our religion as the Sh'ma itself are the words which follow immediately thereafter in our prayers. The traditional Jew repeats this phrase three times daily, but it is in fact, the common heritage of all who would live the religious way of life. The verse comes from the sixth chapter of the Book of Deuteronomy. "And thou shalt love the Lord, Thy God, with all thy heart and with all thy soul, and with all thy might."

Sometimes I feel that too many of us are over-concerned for God's love of us. When everything goes well with us in our personal affairs we complacently reflect that we are enjoying the full benefits of God's love. The likelihood is that when trouble and sorrow and pain take their turn with us, as they do in every life, we then conclude that somehow God's love has been withdrawn, though we find it almost impossible to discover why. The Bible suggests that such questioning may be fruitless. In fact, since our ability to understand God's ways is so very limited, we would do well to turn our minds to matters more completely within our grasp. We should be concerned with our love for God, something over which we have control, something within our powers of comprehension, and something we can guide and direct in the working out of our daily existence. Isn't it much the same with the love we experience in our family circles? It is one of earth's holiest joys to feel the love of our dear ones poured out on us. But in this process we are passive, we are the receivers whose only fit response is to appreciate that which is received. Family love is not a matter of exchange and barter. The home is not a marketplace where affection is traded for affection. Affection can only be met by appreciation. The ideal home is where each person loves and that love is accepted gratefully. But it is not the part of any individual to make demands of someone else's love for him. This is bound to bring unhappiness. We can only make demands upon our own selves, to appreciate what we receive and to bestow our affection as bountifully as we are able to do it.

So, too, with the idea of Love and God, we must appreciate what we receive from Him. But our primary concern is to give Him our Love with all our heart, and with all our soul, and with all our might. Translated into the language of our own day, this loving of God is the equivalent of "being religious." There may be various ways of expressing our religion, through worship, through ceremonies, through daily conduct. The religious man, at best, combines all these. But any or all of these expressions would be meaningless without the sentiment in one's heart which we call "love of God."

Remember that the prayer goes on to say, "You shall teach the love of God diligently to your children and speak of it in your house and on the way, in every waking moment. Keep it ever before your eyes, even write it on the doorposts of your house." Religion, in other words, must be a constant and unfailing factor in our lives. It is not a once-a-week concern, certainly not a once-a-year matter. It must be a daily force with us. Our whole outlook on life must be dominated by it. Every word and action of ours must be guided by the love of God. In times of crisis such as we are in today, this is not less true, but more true. We have become almost callous to the word "critical" as applied to our day and situation. No description less serious is warranted. To say that America today stands on the brink of war is already an understatement. We have become full participants, except for two considerations. The first and more obvious is that our men are not yet in battle. The second and more important is that our people are not aware how deeply they are already involved. They still think this may be a war to the last British soldier, by which time England shall win her famous final battle of victory, and we can settle back to domestic concerns once again. A more serious case of self-delusion and wishful thinking can scarcely be imagined. We publicly proclaim the Allied cause to be our own, then expect a miracle out of Greece, or Turkey or North Africa or Russia or Britain itself, to keep us at peace at our sound and safe distance over here. We still have not made up our minds how safe America can be with the rest of the world Nazi-dominated.

Here is where a clear decision must be reached without delay. Then two specific alternatives would confront us: either we pull ourselves entirely into our own shells—if possible with the rest of the Americans, or we stop our half-hearted aid to Britain and openly enter the conflict with every force and energy at our command. I, for one, would never advocate such action, not because with Lindbergh I should be afraid of defeat, but because I believe adding war to war is not the road to peace. However, a frank admission of America's true position would at least have the merit of being honest and courageous, as against our present half-way measures which strike me as both dishonest and cowardly. I say again that the evil represented by Nazism must be resisted by all to whom decency and religion are dear. As to the method of resistance I cannot believe that religion can sanction the war-and-violence method, but if this is the method America has endorsed with her promise of "all out" aid to Britain, we only delude ourselves that it can be "short of war." With the passing of the Lend-Lease Bill, America threw herself into the war, and she is in it deeply at this very moment.

To love God and to contradict His law against destroying human life, whether by our machines or our soldiers, is the strange position in which we find ourselves today. Telling ourselves we murder in self-defense makes the murder no less a sin. Sin it will remain even if crowned by victory, sin that falls upon all of us like the bombs of modern battle themselves upon combatant and non-combatant alike, upon interventionist and pacifist alike. There is simply no gainsaying this fact, no matter how unpleasant it happens to be. At the same time, even when one's country is in war, the totality of living is not consumed by the war. There are still vast areas of life where the love of God can still be the dominant force within us. There is still the earning of our daily bread, the rearing of families, the education of children. There is still a whole realm of experience calling upon us for love and truth, for justice and kindness, for mercy and gentleness. The very existence of war is a challenge that these virtues be preserved. Yet the very existence of war and its glorification of physical courage is a challenge that spiritual courage be kept alive in this bleak world.

The power of God has been beaten down before. Other periods in history have witnessed smashing victories for the powers of Evil. Jewish thought has always held that there is an inclination to do good and an inclination to do evil in every human being. It is our moral duty to be so governed by the love of God in our hearts that our inclination to evil is controlled, is suppressed, is entirely dominated by our inclination to do good. This is the principal tenet in Jewish ethics, and just as it applies to our personal lives, so it must apply to the society in whose midst we live. The world as a whole has far to go before it sees this realized on the largest plane. But it persists as the dream, the aspiration of all religion and so long as the Love of God remains enshrined in human hearts and embodies in human actions, that dream may still be realized. It is for us, then, to love God with all our heart and soul and might. Thus we can be confident that the victory of tomorrow will be ours.

Religion in a Democracy at War

War is a terrible thing. War is a crime against humanity. War is a cardinal sin. Men have realized this for many hundreds of years. Religion has emphasized this with increasing fervor from the days of Isaiah up to the present hour. In fact, the voice of organized religion has spoken almost incessantly in behalf of peace, and has helped to bring civilized society a long distance from those days in human history when war was considered glorious, the principal activity of the truly manly man, and the ideal occasion to bring out all of the finest, most creative forces in the individual personality.

Naturally, war with its bloodshed and destruction is the antithesis of religion's highest teachings. And yet history demonstrates clearly that when war comes, religion has never stood completely aloof from it. Twenty-five years ago, a rabbi in Philadelphia set out, in his doctor's thesis, to show how completely religion opposed the recurring epidemic of warfare. He was forced to conclude that although religion may consistently condemn fighting, religious leaders, both clergymen and laymen, almost invariably endorse it, once it is under way. In fact, leaders of religion have frequently added fuel to the fire once the conflagration had been started.

Today, there are more teachers of religion than in any other crisis of history who maintain their opposition to war. To mention the names of John Hayes Holmes, George Buttrick, Allan Knight Chalmers, Henry Emerson Fosdick, Methodist Bishop Paul Kern and Walter Van Kirk, Episcopal Bishop W. Appleton Lawrence and William Mitchell is simply to indicate the best known of the liberals in leading American pulpits who reaffirm their pacifist convictions, even now that the nation is at war. Literally hundreds of other ministers in almost all denominations stand with them at this hour.

We who take this stand do so with anxious hearts and agonized spirits. We condone in not the least wise the brutal attacks of the Japanese government upon American armed forces and civilians. We view with the utmost abhorrence all that the Nazi and Fascist powers have done to enslave the peoples of Europe. We completely oppose the whole philosophy and program of the Axis forces. And we dearly love this country, her people and institutions and ideals. We know full well that nothing we can say or do can prevent the ever increasing scale of bloodshed and destruction in this present conflict.

Yet in view of the teachings of our faiths, in view of our own confirmed convictions, and in view of the dictates of our conscience, we find that speaking in the name of religion we cannot bless, sanction or support the method of war, even though the cause appears to be so justified in the eyes of our fellow-countrymen. We are compelled to call war the unmitigated evil we see it to be, even when our nation feels itself thrust into the employment of that evil. And we feel called upon, at least by our own conduct of non-participation, to represent before a free people the ideal of non-violence which all civilized men must ultimately not only espouse but put into universal practice.

There have been ministers of religion in Great Britain holding the same point of view, and charting the same course of action ever since war began in September, 1939. They have found themselves very busy in the many fields of service, aside from actual military affairs, in which their consciences permitted them to take part and they have set us a goodly example. Pacifists in England are working hard to save the lives of civilians, becoming masters of first-aid skills and readily volunteering for such dangerous work as removing unexploded bombshells often at the risk of their own lives. Their stand is not only a negative one but involves positive service of merciful humanitarian character.

At the same time, we, who cannot support war by abandoning or setting aside our deeply rooted principles, have no intention whatsoever of obstructing or interfering with the decisions and the program of the government. We respect the point of view of our fellow-citizens to whom war presents itself as a patriotic duty. We believe them to be honest and sincere when they claim that though they detest the use of armed force it has now become a necessary evil in order to preserve a free way of life.

Aside from the minority of which I have spoken, by and

large religion as a whole, the vast majority of ministers and official organizations of churches and synagogues, here as in England, has thrown its entire influence in support of governmental action. Many pulpits are urging volunteers for the armed forces and for military defense at home. Many ministers have either enlisted in fighting units or put themselves under military orders as chaplains. Others are promoting government defense borrowing. Some are going to extremes to whip up warlike emotional reactions among the general populace in the name of public morale. There are even those who are sowing seeds of intolerance and hatred in their desire to augment the fighting spirit of the people of the land.

Just as we can find all kinds of religious expressions, ranging in variety down to the level of Holy Rollers and Voodoo, so we find those who completely lose sight of spiritual values in their hysteria over the country's fate.

All the while the real role of religion in a democracy at war stares us in the face. The program is a large and hard one, but it is one that must be carried through:

1st. Religion must keep alive in the hearts and minds of Americans the ideals of our country and the reverence of Almighty God, lest we arrive at victory over the enemy only to find him victorious over us.

2nd. Religion must service with all its resources the spiritual and moral welfare of the people at home, and the boys who are away. At home parents and wives and children find themselves with new needs for the service religion can render, and must not be left without religion's customary ministrations, educational activities and worship. For the boys who are away, religion must support the U.S.O., the United Service Organization, and thus help provide for the social and moral care of those who have been removed from their normal environment.

3rd. Religion must be particularly concerned for every cause of mercy such as the Red Cross, the care of prisoners of war, and all appeals for relieving distress and suffering from whatever corner of the earth they may come. Not only the giving but the doing of active personal service must be encouraged in the name of mercy and humanity.

4th. Religion must prevent the growth of destructive hate, lest it continue its ravages long after a new peace is established. There must be understanding of and fairness toward all minorities in America, as well as restraint and sympathy with regard to the millions of men, women and children in enemy lands. If viciousness and revenge get into our blood, we will only create new wars that our children's children will have to suffer.

5th. Religion must hold before the world the confidence that right and justice will prevail. This is no mere hope but a positive knowledge in the light of our faith in God. And,

6th. Religion must guide the developing of democracy's peace aims. If the President is ever to carry out his promise of "winning the peace" after the war, he must have the direction and guidance of religious teachers upon which to build. That is no last-minute task for when a war is ended. Already in England, the heads of all religious bodies have set forth principles upon which the new world must be founded. These are called "The 10 Points of the British Churches." Here in America our Central Conference of American Rabbis, the Federal Council of Churches, and other official religious groups have issued similar and almost identical proclamations. This is only the beginning of religion's bounden duty to make certain that the new peace is a lasting peace, because it rests on the solid rock of the laws of God, is built out of the materials of Justice and Truth and Love, and joining all nations together as members of one family under God's Fatherhood.

Friends, it is not the business of religion, whose ideal is mercy and kindliness and gentleness in human behavior, to engage in war. Neither can religion lock itself up in an ivory tower of isolation and indifference once war has come upon us. Even when the bombs are falling on us there is godly work to be done. It must be done with persistence and devotion, even dedication, by clergy and laymen alike, if the light of civilization is not to be blacked-out.

Pacifism in Its Ethical and Spiritual Implications

This is the first time I have ever addressed a pacifist organization, though I have long been a member of two or three, and I feel at this moment like a lamb newly thrown into a den of lions. It is not that I am preoccupied by your ferocity. To the contrary, I am persuaded you are domesticated. I am merely embarrassed by the difference of our size, the austerity of your appearance, and the naiveté of innocence with which my views are likely to impress you.

It is considered good form at the beginning of an address to convince one's hearers that the speaker is preeminently qualified to do justice to his subject. What one may have to offer is said to require this rhetorical stimulation, this comforting assurance and motivation for listening. Who has the time or the patience to waste in the company of the amateur, the tyro, the scarcely initiated?

Yet, in the name of honesty, I must deprive you—without further ado—of any delusion you may be experiencing as to my competence tonight. I have been a pacifist for nearly 17 years— which fact alone, and in splendid isolation—accounts for the temerity that permitted my accepting your gracious invitation to appear before you. But I am confident that there is no single individual present who does not know more than do I about pacifism—its history, philosophy, current developments—nay more, its ethical and spiritual implications which I am asked to discuss. This is not a pretense of humility on my part. It is a simple, candid confession, and is motivated by selfish considerations. I am sensitive concerning my ignorance of pacifist literature, my neglect of familiarity with pacifist dialectics, and my merely tangential relationship to the active movement of which you are all so effective a part. The selfishness I have in this regard resided in the vanity I insist upon, of making my ignorance and lack of authority and qualification manifestly clear, before you have occasion to call it to my attention.

I could enlarge upon this theme to the point of your complete and consuming boredom, for as a conscientious objector to war I have something of a conscience, and I am strongly convinced that no one has the right—intellectually—to take the stand of pacifism, and yet be as ill-prepared as I am to expound its merits, establish its glories, and devastate—beyond refute—all arguments raised to contradict it. We pacifists are handicapped in the efficacious propagation of our cause, through adherents such as myself, who are not at the same time worthy and forthright advocates. I do not recall ever winning a single convert. There may have been a non-believer here and there who has been disturbed in his complacency, who has had his faith in violence slightly shaken by reason of my position, my intransigence, the example of my mulish stubbornness, but I have never had the joy of enlisting a proselyte whom I have inspired. In the summer of 1932, under the auspices of the American Friends Service Committee, I made 53 pacifist speeches in the towns and villages of southwest Ohio, and the only person I was able to convince was myself. "The mountain labored and brought forth a mouse." I also convinced myself that as an evangelist I was "dead-weight" to the movement. Perhaps the less I said and the more I tried to live, the greater contribution I might be able to make. This was rationalization, pure and simple. Pacifism needs its battlers, its staunch proponents, its fiery zealots, its indomitable fanatics as much as, if not more than, others of God's causes. And the tools we must use are logic and reason, demonstrable facts and ardent, irresistible persuasion. This demands knowledge and the application of specific techniques, no less than personal conviction, courage, enthusiasm and selfless dedication. More power to those who are formidably informed and impressively aggressive!

All pretenses and deceptions disposed of, I can now attempt to face the subject assigned to me, to put forward various subjective views and to discourse *ex cathedra*, for whatever small value might be anticipated to such an approach. Pacifism, as I understand it, is the rejection by individuals of the use of violence and bloodshed in resolving international disputes, and the concomitant compulsion to promote world peace through the abolition of war as an instrumentality of nations and men, under any and all circumstances. Recently, in the local press, pacifism was called (William Hessler, Inquirer, March 17, 1949) "A blind revulsion from war." Perhaps nothing could be more misleading than such a description, for pacifism is, if anything, peculiarly perceptive and clear-sighted. It achieves its clarity of vision by purifying the mind and heart of their most deceitful delusions, and conditioning them—out of the ethical and spiritual insights of the past, as well as by a common-sensce understanding of history and human experience—to look upon present-day realities without hindrance or obstruction or interference. By reason of religious conviction, or because of other humanitarian considerations, we see every personality as sacred and inviolable. If the willful taking of a single human life is wrong, we recognize that the willful taking of human lives to the nth number, is wrong to the nth degree. If we abhor and refrain from the one, we abhor and refrain from the other, all the more positively and affirmatively. On the other hand, we see war as the most conspicuous violation of the fundamental moral imperative: "Thou shalt not murder." And on the other hand, we understand the hope of mankind to reside in the wisdom communicated by the prophet Zechariah, "Not by might nor yet by power, but by My spirit, saith the Lord." Therefore pacifists assert, "We will not engage in war, neither will we aid or abet it. At the same time we will do everything in our power to establish the spirit of

God within human affairs, as a substitute for war and for all other forms of might and power which obviously contradict or militate against the spirit of God."

It is clear that pacifism, as it is understood today, requires in the first place, a personal stand that is taken by an individual regarding his own relationship to the war process. To the extent that our conscience is satisfied, we "wash our hands" of the "monster of iniquity" and declare that it is not for us. Our soul shall not be tainted by any involvement on our own part. We will be among the pure and unblemished with regard to at least this one great corrupting factor in human experience. We "shall not follow after the multitude to do evil." In the choice that we have as free men and women, we will elect the way of isolation, of "no traffic," or abstinence.

As we do this, we reduce the number of individuals whose moral and spiritual records are besmirched by the particular brand of immorality that war engenders. We are decreasing sin, at least quantitatively, in the world. We are asserting man's right to peace, and his protest against human destruction. We are patterning ourselves after one facet of the personalities of certain of the most exemplary spiritual geniuses that history has ever known. We are refraining from contributing or adding to the calamitous effects which are so inevitable an outcome of war. We are setting an example which, if the entire world followed, would of necessity bring about the end of war for all time. We are taking the sixth commandment seriously, and being mindful of some of the most exalted teachings ever uttered to men. We are fellows with Whittier in crying abroad: "O men and brothers! Let that voice be heard: War fails, try peace! Put up the useless sword."

Insofar as we recognize such merit to exist in our refusing truck with war, we pacifists find ourselves upon firm ground, morally and spiritually. But insofar as we exaggerate these merits, or allow them to assume undue significance, or pride ourselves in our superior virtue, or delight in the sacrifices we must make, or imagine that we have thus resolved the major issues of war and peace—to any such extent we are minimizing, even undermining our cause, and standing upon no more than quicksand, morally and spiritually. Isaiah knew that it is never enough to "cease to do evil." He was compelled to add in the same breath, "learn to do well."

I, for one, have no doubt but that we do well by ceasing to do evil, but it is only a meager beginning of the well-doing, the creative, constructive contribution we must make, as devotees of peace, to the warless world that we envision. It seems to me that our position is tenable, not so much by its "sweet reasonableness" as by the demand it makes upon us to be builders of the better tomorrow.

There are others who have found considerable satisfaction in what might be called the parochial interests of pacifism: working for better laws respecting conscientious objectors, serving those in the movement who are suffering most painfully from its penalties, (so to speak), erecting and perfecting organizations of all who subscribe to our ideals, and striving to achieve the maximum of consistency in applying their principles to peace-time situations. Many of these labors are inevitable, even indispensable, but they must never deflect us from the main courses which are incumbent upon us to travel. The first of these is the orientation of our personalities in keeping with the conviction that evil is to be resolved by other than violent means. The second is participation in the vanguard of the preventers of World War III. And the third is enlistment—even in the rank and file—to so order human society as to eliminate the causes of all future wars. A few words about each of these objectives may not be amiss.

Many of you at this season recall the words of that great American hymn, "As he died to make men holy, let us die to make men free." I shall never forget the impression made upon my own thinking when I first heard those thrilling words interpreted in the pacifist sense: we are not told to *kill* to make men free, but to be willing to *die*. How much more, we cannot help but ask, must we be willing to *live* to make men free? Very few, if any among us, can be called a professional pacifist in that we devote our entire time and talents and energies to the cause that is so dear to our hearts. In our varied occupations, in our family experiences, in our personal relationships at every level, is there a conscious effort to translate pacifism into daily blessings? Do we live upon a plane that is characterized by the abrogation of belligerence and violence, on the one hand, and the affirmation of righteousness and justice and truth and love, on the other? Pacifism should be at work within us, should be revealed in our every word and action, if we take it as seriously as we prefer to think we do.

Our second obligation is to prevent the outbreak, if it has not already started, of a third world-wide cataclysm of nations, or if it has started, to arrest its development into an open conflict. I suppose that few issues would find us so divided as the "what" and "how" to achieve just this, and I would not be so rash as to outline a program in the hope that it would meet with anything like a general acceptance. But I submit that the very proposition itself, that this must be one of our primary and immediate concerns is taken all too lightly, is viewed all too casually. Permit me the heresy of remarking that neither propagating our faith in the rightness of pacifism and its ultimate triumph, nor rendering humanitarian services to peoples everywhere in need—however magnificently inspiring as well as beneficent such service may be—nor exerting our every effort to reduce the armaments of our own and friendly nations—none of these and kindred endeavors upon which we lovers of peace expend so much of our powers, from which we derive such marked satisfaction and in which we appear to repose so many of our hopes; none of these seems to me to offer genuine promise for precluding the unspeakable devastation of a new war. Eyes fixed upon the farthest horizons, we dare not miss the "main chance" close at hand. Hyperopia may be as calamitous as myopia. And a tide that requires a Boulder Dam cannot be stemmed by sandbags! We must be the last to succumb to a fatalism—so utterly immoral—that implies we shall be justified or our position vindicated in some "far-off divine event"—and the devil take the foremost! Russia and

America must be kept from fighting, and unless we help to effect a reconciliation that means the surrender of neither what the Western powers consider to be *their* understanding of freedom nor of what the Soviet Union considers to be *its* understanding of freedom, we shall be guilty, as "accessories after the fact," in a globe-shattering Armageddon, not the least result of which may well be setting back of the clock of pacifism by many hundreds, even thousands of years.

This should be enough of a moral and spiritual burden for us to carry: making pacifism manifest in our personal relations and stopping the war at our doorstep. Unless we are successful in the first, we differ little from others who abhor war, and thank God their number is legion! And unless we are successful in the second, our light will be dimmed in a world that is shrouded in darkness. But we know that yet another duty devolves upon us; the creation of the state of human affairs from which the causes of war shall be removed, and in which the economic, political, social and spiritual foundations of genuine peace shall be firmly established. This is our long-term objective, but its implementation is not to be postponed.

> Heaven is not reached at a single bound;
> But we build the ladder by which we rise
> From the lowly earth to the vaulted skies,
> And we mount to its summit round by round.
> —Josiah G. Holland, Graduation

Again, I would not presume to prescribe the one formula by which our sick world will be cured of those virulent poisons that cripple mankind periodically with war. However, to be in the forefront of the physicians who are manfully laboring, not only for immediate therapy but for systematic sanitation and immunization in human society—this, it seems to me—is an inescapable obligation we take upon ourselves as pacifists. The magnitude of the task is enough to overwhelm us! Some measure of strength and encouragement comes to us out of the wisdom of the first-century religious teacher (Rabbi Tarfon, *Abot* II, 20) who said, "It is not thy duty to complete the work, but neither art thou free to desist from it."

Everyone wants peace. We know that wanting it alone, never achieves it. Pacifism commits us to action, to translate the desires of our hearts into personality values, into reconciling the differences which are now leading nations into a new abyss, into building the warless world, without which the human race will not long survive. Our spiritual and moral advantage is in our commitment to God and to the good. We have to prove ourselves worthy of that commitment.

Selection XI

This final selection is the contribution of Andy Mager, the first Jew in American history to be indicted and convicted for draft resistance. For the offense of refusing to register for the draft, Andy was sentenced in January 1985 to a three-year term, with six months to be served in "a jail-type institution" and the remainder suspended. As of this writing, Andy has completed his prison sentence, with the thirty-month period of probation looming ahead for him. The Jewish Peace Fellowship, joined by peace activists everywhere, supports and salutes him.

Andy's sister, Amy Mager, was an outstanding student at Brandeis University, class of 1985. On campus, I had the distinct pleasure of having her as a student, early in her undergraduate days, in my Conscientious Objection seminar. By the end of her campus career, Amy came to reject conscientious objection as an option which she considers to be unfairly accessible to the educated and advantaged alone. On that score, Amy and I disagree. Conscientious objection, an honorable prerogative in my view, represents the legal way for a person of conscience to refuse military service. At the same time, as COs assume the responsibility of exposing and sensitizing others of various socioeconomic classes to this legal alternative to serving in the armed forces, conscientious objection becomes increasingly accessible to all strata. This is, indeed, the goal: to educate all classes in conscientious objection, to spread the work of nonviolence, and to rear generation upon generation of objectors to war.

Be that as it may, Andy Mager refused to register for the draft, for which he was harshly penalized. In addressing his supporters before the trial, according to Carolyn Toll's reports ("The Courage to Resist: Andy Mager's Story," *Fellowship*, March 1985; "The Courage of a Resister," *Genesis 2*, 16, no. 6 [April 1985/Nisan 5745]), Andy "announced he was going to recite a poem entitled 'Blessed Is the Match.' He told the crowd the story of Hannah Senesh, the young Zionist who gave her life trying to save her fellow Hungarian Jews by leaving the safety of Palestine to parachute into Nazi-occupied Hungary in 1944 to rescue them from the coming deportations. Andy said he was inspired by her example of courage in confronting evil and considered his action an attempt to follow her tradition."

During the trial itself, according to Toll's court-covering account, Andy launched into his eloquent self-defense with these words: "I am a Jew," he began softly. "I look back on World War II with horror at the millions of my people who were killed. Under the Nuremberg accords initiated by the U.S. following that war, many Nazi war criminals were sent to prison for obeying orders. Under principles VI and VII of these accords, I have an obligation not to participate in the 'planning, preparation, initiation or waging of war in violation of international treaties, accords and agreements.' And this is true even if it means that I must disobey a law of my own country."

He then continued:

Registration is the first step from the civilian to the military world. By registering, I am in essence participating in the uses which the US government has chosen for its military force. I believe that based on Article VI of the Constitution, which says that all treaties are the supreme law of the land, I have a responsibility not to register, in order to not be complicit in US violations of international law. I believe that my duty to register is negated by my belief that the US government is involved in violations of international law in its policies relating to Nicaragua. Those policies violate the following treaties: the United Nations Charter, the Charter of the Organization of American States, the Inter-American Treaty on the Rights and Duties of

States and the anti-war Treaty of Non-Aggression and Concilia-
tion. The US is party to all these agreements, which recognize
that no country has the right to intervene in the internal affairs of
another country.

Several courts during the Vietnam era said that the link
between registering or being inducted and US violations of
international law was too tenuous to allow this type of defense
to be presented. As a result, the war continued and more
American soldiers and Vietnamese soldiers and civilians were
killed. When will the courts hear the issue? Must we wait for
50,000 American lives and countless Nicaraguan lives to be lost
before the US government is held accountable for its actions?
The reasonableness of these beliefs is greatly enhanced by the
World Court's decision to hear the case of Nicaragua versus the
United States. Despite the statements by the US government
that the World Court has no jurisdiction, the Court has decided
that Nicaragua has a strong enough case that it should go to trial.

These international agreements among nations seek to establish humane ways for people to relate to each other. Unfortunately these agreements tend to be ignored by the US, as well as
other countries. As I learned of these treaties I recognized that if
they were followed, countries would be able to turn away from a
reliance on military force and weapons of destruction and instead to focus on human development.

I truly believe that individual people must take risks in our
own lives in order to change the world around us. Appeals to the
government to change are simply not enough. Refusing to
register is in many ways a very personal decision. I don't claim
that it is what everyone should do. But the government passed a
law requiring that I fill out a card, in case they want to send me
to war. It gives my consent and participation in preparation for
war. Not only do I believe that I could not in good conscience fill
out that card, but that under the Nuremberg Accords I have a
responsibility not to do so. I believe the government's ability to
wage wars around the world and violate the treaties it has signed
depends upon the cooperation of the people they expect to do
the fighting for them.

I believe that my resistance to this war is part of a long
tradition of social change—which includes the Boston Tea Party,
the underground railroad helping slaves to escape, the unioniza-

tion of the labor movement, the civil rights lunch counter sit-ins, the abolition of child labor laws and the withdrawal of United States troops from Vietnam. All of these efforts helped gain a greater degree of freedom and democracy in this country. Many of the people involved were called traitors, communists and lawbreakers. They were jailed, beaten and sometimes killed. In retrospect, how do we look at them? These lawbreakers included: Thomas Paine, Harriet Tubman, Susan B. Anthony, Martin Luther King and many others who are recognized as people who helped make this country a better place for all.

In court I am told that I am in the wrong place, that this isn't the place for moral and political issues to be addressed. We are at a time in history where if we don't prevent war it may destroy our world. I don't claim that my individual act of refusing to register will by itself end war. But it is a step. It's the response of a concerned person reacting to a world which in many ways seems to be tottering at the edge. I ask you to join me in exploring how we will end the war.

In the following short article, distributed nationally by the Jewish Peace Fellowship, Andy Mager continues to relate his Jewish heritage to his courageous stand as a conscientious draft resister.

As I prepare for my trial for refusing to register for the draft, I often question how my beliefs developed. I wonder why I am willing to risk five years in prison for refusing to sign my name on a piece of paper. Much of this questioning leads me to reflect on the connections between my upbringing in the Jewish culture and religion, and the work in which I am involved for peace and justice.

I was raised in an upper middle-class Jewish family in the suburbs of New York City. I started going to religious school in the second grade. My family belonged to a Reform congregation. I remember feeling the religion as somewhat separate from my everyday life. I, along with my brother and sisters went to religious school, and the whole family went to Temple on major holidays. We had a Seder each year. I learned about the oppression of the Jewish people—from slavery in Egypt to the Diaspora, World War II, and continued anti-semitism today. I felt pride that the State of Israel could be a refuge for Jews in a dangerous world.

In addition to the more "religious" aspects of being raised as a Jew, I grew up in a Jewish culture (although it was certainly a watered down, assimilated version). Education was stressed as a virtue. Part of this included learning to make informed decisions based on my own knowledge and feelings. I recall a deep anger at the treatment of Jewish people and a feeling that no one should be treated in this way.

I think that these are the roots of the work I do today. No one should be denied the fundamental control of his or her destiny and the right to make the decisions which affect that destiny. This is true whether an individual is Jewish, black American, Arab or Palestinian.

I believe that war is one of the most fundamental examples of inhumanity. The tremendous quantity of nuclear weapons and conventional weapons of mass destruction possessed by the United States, the U.S.S.R. and other countries has made war a threat to all of life on our earth. By refusing to register for the draft, I am saying, in as clear a way as I am able, that I will not participate in this destruction.

My great grandparents came to this country at the turn of the century during a time of massive Jewish migration. Since that time, Jews have been active in every movement for peace and justice. From Emma Goldman to Jerry Rubin, Jews have participated in the labor movement, the civil rights movement, the women's movement, the peace movement and other struggles too numerous to list.

I see myself as part of this tradition. It is a tradition of Jews who recognize the extent of our oppression as Jewish people. And in responding to that oppression we have come to realize that the struggle for our own liberation is intimately connected to the struggles of other oppressed people. This is a lesson we must learn if we are ever to live in a world free of anti-semitism.

ABOUT THE AUTHOR

Rabbi Albert S. Axelrad serves as B'nai B'rith Hillel Director and Chaplain at Brandeis University, a position he has occupied since his rabbinical ordination in 1965. He has been a member of the National Executive Committee of the Jewish Peace Fellowship and a long-time peace activist and counselor on the draft and conscientious objection. Rabbi Axelrad's other books are: *Meditations of a Maverick Rabbi*, Rossel Books, Chappaqua, NY, 1985 and *Refusenik: Voices of Hope and Struggle*, Wyndham Hall, Bristol, Indiana, 1985.